The Way of the Traveler

Making Every Trip a Journey of Self-Discovery

Other Books by Joseph Dispenza

The Magical Realism of Alyce Frank
Live Better Longer: The Parcells Center Seven-Step Plan for Health and Longevity
The Serigraphs of Doug West
Will Shuster: A Santa Fe Legend
The House of Alarcon
Advertising the American Woman
Freeze Frame: A History of the American Film
Re-Runs
Forgotten Patriot

The Way of the Traveler

Making Every Trip a Journey of Self-Discovery

Joseph Dispenza

JOHN MUIR PUBLICATIONS
SANTA FE, NEW MEXICO

This book is dedicated to Michael Charles Herbert.

❦

John Muir Publications, P.O. Box 613, Santa Fe, New Mexico 87504

Copyright © 1999 by John Muir Publications
First edition. First printing September 1999.

Book design by Janine Lehmann
Illustrations by Aaron Bohrer
Cover images: Top right—Robb Helfrick;
top left—Francis Travers;
bottom left—Janine Lehmann;
bottom right—Aaron Bohrer
Interior photos: page 7—Angelo Cavalli/Leo de Wys Inc.;
pages 29, 51, 73, 95—Janine Lehmann

Library of Congress Cataloging-in-Publication Data
Dispenza, Joseph, 1942–
The way of the traveler: making every trip a journey
of self-discovery / Joseph Dispenza
p.   cm.
Includes bibliographical references.
ISBN 1-56261-488-6
1. Travel—Religious aspects. I. Title.
BL628.8.D57   1999
291.3'5—dc21   99-28334
CIP

Distributed to the book trade by
Publishers Group West, Berkeley, California

contents

contents

Once more on my adventure brave and new.
—Robert Browning, "Rabbi Ben Ezra"

Introduction

All travel is inner travel.

A journey is always about going from where we are now to another place. We go literally, but we can also travel figuratively as we search for another, higher level of consciousness.

Seen this way, all our travel has a spiritual character.

And, in this way, all our travel is sacred.

Every time we take a trip, we have an opportunity to expand our awareness and thus to grow spiritually. Travel, undertaken with mindfulness, can be a powerful vehicle for personal transformation.

Whether we are going around the world or merely across town, we can enter the exhilarating adventure of the archetypal, or universal, journey, and we can experience the profound inner metamorphosis that it promises. Conscious travel elevates the process of our journey and enriches our spiritual life.

The literature of all cultures speaks of life as a journey. The great heroes of mythology left the comforts of home and embarked on epic expeditions into the unknown. The accounts of their travels, celebrated in song and passed down through the centuries, form the wisdom of the ages. In myth, the journey of life is an adventure of unparalleled drama and excitement calling forth courage, integrity, generosity, and endurance—and giving back a deep spiritual understanding.

Inspirational literature often refers to the spiritual life as the journey of the soul. The seeker quits the everyday routine and travels inward, into the undiscovered country, to find the divine presence at the heart of his or her being. Through meditation, prayer, and other spiritual practices, the searcher for spiritual knowledge makes a pilgrimage to the divinity within—a brave journey requiring the same virtues with which the heroes of myth armed themselves. The end of the journey for both heroes and saints is enlightenment.

If we look at the pattern of the journey as it has come down to us over eons, we see some distinct phases. The first is that of imagining the journey—dreaming about taking the road to another place. Next is preparation: deciding what is to be taken along and what is to remain behind. The third phase involves making the journey itself, with all its serendipitous encounters and amazing unfoldings. After that is the homecoming. And finally, to complete the experience, the traveler recounts the tale of the journey.

This book follows the classical phases of a journey and adds to them a spiritual dimension. It begins with the dream of travel. We are restless for movement. We think of leaving where we are and going away, and we imagine what we might encounter on the road to new discoveries.

When the dream starts to become reality, we actively prepare for the trip. Now a host of choices must be made. What mode of transportation will we use? What belongings need to be packed and brought with us, and what can be left at home? Who will care for what we leave behind?

At last, we embark on the journey itself. The adventures of this trip are amazing, enlarging. We never could have imagined or planned for these people, these sights, these experiences, these openings of the heart.

The journey is over and we return home. But things seem to have changed. In our absence life went on, and we were not a part of it. We are larger, somehow, from our travels, and we see farther. Slowly, all that once was familiar becomes familiar again—but uplifted to something higher.

We close the book of our journey upon the retelling of it. We gather our family, our friends, and show pictures, relate stories, play the music of the place. In this way the journey reaches completion. The lessons learned are passed to those we love.

Travel becomes a spiritual experience when we are conscious at every moment that our physical transportation from place to place has a metaphysical counterpart. Understanding that, the road leads us to an encounter with the "stranger" at the heart of the journey—we meet ourselves, transformed.

This is the way of the traveler.

I have written this book as a collection of reflections on the spiritual aspects of travel. Each reflection is followed by a simple activity that brings that aspect to life, then by a meditation, or affirmation, to help you seal the thought and make it yours.

The activities in the book are only suggestions—you may come up with your own ways to animate the reflections I have provided. But I highly recommend that you add as many "mindful" activities as possible to your travel experience. Even small actions of a spiritual nature, you will find, can elevate your travel and bring to it the richness of a sacred event.

In the Middle Ages, pilgrims undertaking a long journey to an important hallowed shrine were given a book of prayers and reflections for spiritual support on the road. The small book was called a *vade mecum*—literally, in Latin, "go with me."

Chaucer's Canterbury pilgrims carried these little volumes to strengthen their resolve as they made their progress through the countryside. Don Quixote kept one in his tunic when he ventured out, lance in hand, onto the Spanish plains. Joan of Arc tucked one under her armor, close to her heart, as she galloped into battle.

This book is meant to be that for you—a store of spiritual provisions for your journey in the outer world, which is the road, finally, to self-discovery.

I hope this will be your *vade mecum*.

Take only memories. Leave nothing but footprints.

—Chief Seattle

The Journal of Feelings

Keeping a journal while on the road is a time-honored tradition. Some of the world's most famous travel books are journals kept by observant and articulate travelers. Many of them are deeply personal records of visiting exotic places. The more personal the journals, the more of "the spirit of the place" they offer us.

As you begin to move toward your own expedition of discovery, consider keeping a journal. But instead of a simple "today I did this, tomorrow I will see that" kind of journal, think in terms of drafting a journal of your feelings.

A journal of feelings is a record of how you felt about the people and things you encountered along the path of your journey.

Committing to paper the vast inventory of emotions you will experience during travel serves several purposes. First, it allows you to identify and anchor your feelings. Were you angry at something or someone—elated at a turn of events? Emotions come swiftly when you are away from home and exploring new worlds. Without a way of describing them clearly, gathering them together, and fixing them, they will be lost to the winds.

Next, keeping a journal of feelings makes your trip profoundly more personal. It is one thing to experience a new place in a standard travel brochure way and quite another to be able to react emotionally to it in your own unique manner. The Coliseum? Not just a picture on a poster. You could hear the roar of hungry lions, the clanging swords of gladiators, the thunderous cheers of the crowd; it sent a chill of excitement through you.

Finally, a journal of feelings elevates your trip from a mere sightseeing excursion to an archetypal hero's journey. Keeping a chronicle of your feelings gives you the opportunity to trace the movements of your heart as you make your way. It transforms a trip of discovery into a journey of self-discovery.

Your journal of feelings will help lift your trip into a sacred spiritual experience.

Part One

THE DREAM OF THE JOURNEY

Beyond the East the sunrise,
beyond the West the sea.
And East and West the wander-thirst
that will not let me be.

Gerald Gould, Wander-Thirst

Nothing happens unless first a dream.
—Carl Sandburg

The Call to Journey

The urge to travel starts as a far-off yearning to change where we are. We can somehow sense it, the call of the unconscious to move into the outer world. Listening to the call of that still, small voice deep within is the first step of the journey.

Our journey is born in a kind of sacred restlessness.

In his poem "The Explorer," Rudyard Kipling calls the first dreamy inkling of the journey "a voice, as bad as Conscience" that repeats its message night and day: "Something hidden . . . go and find it."

World literature is filled with references to heroes dreaming about journeys before actually embarking on them. Usually a god or goddess appears in a dream and discloses the news that a journey will take place.

The hero's first reaction is often disbelief, followed by apprehension—"Since I had not planned to make a change, how is this to be?" and then, inevitably, "Wait, I cannot go—I am afraid to go." The deity calms the hero with a profusion of assurances and promises to be present invisibly to offer guidance, protection, and solace throughout the trip.

Spiritual texts of all cultures also abound with dreams about journeys. An angel may appear to a sleeping person, announcing the idea of travel. Again, the supernatural being is met with incredulity and uneasiness. And again the person is assured that the journey will be all for the good and that every need along the way will be met with heavenly sustenance.

These illustrations from classical antiquity and from spiritual tradition are not lost on us as we, too, dream about a journey.

Sometimes our dream is just a feeling as we go about our regular routine, a vague discomfort with where we are right now. At other times, it may take a more dramatic appearance. A gentle, otherworldly presence may make itself felt while we sleep or when we are drifting in that hazy territory between sleep and wakefulness.

And the message we receive from that presence is "Depart from this place for a time—the world out there awaits you."

The symbolism of the dream is rich and powerful. It tells us that we can stay here and continue to sleepwalk through our usual paces at home or we can entertain the idea of travel, and with it the possibility of change. It also informs us that if we do answer the call to disengage ourselves from "this place," we will be guided and protected on the way.

The dream of travel announces that each of us has the power to trans-form our lives in a fundamental way.

And it promises that if we pluck up our courage and agree to undertake the journey, the road upon which we travel will lead to self-discovery.

It is no small promise.

In the dream lies the seed of the entire journey. Just as a seed of a tree contains the entire tree and all of its fruit, the dream of travel has within it the whole arc of our trip—from our leave-taking to our homecoming, and everything in between.

No trip is insignificant, the dream seems to tell us. Every time we leave home and go to another place, we open up the possibility of having some-thing wonderful happen to us.

The dream speaks to us, and what it says is this: When we move out of the familiar here and now, we set in motion a series of events that, taken to-gether, bring about changes at the very root of our being.

And it is time to change.

❧ From One Place to Another ❧

A friend told me about what she does whenever she feels the impulse, how-ever slight, to travel. It is really the simplest thing in the world, and, like most simple things, remarkably meaningful.

When she dreams the dream of travel, she consciously moves from one spot to another. That is all! She stands in one place in one room of her house and mentally calls that "home." Then she walks slowly and carefully into another room—to a spot that she has designated "the destination."

To complete the exercise, she walks, just as slowly and carefully, back to her original spot. What could be more elementary than that? And yet, the act of moving from one place to another—from "home" to "destination"—is a microcosmic rendering of the entire journey. It changes your perspective on the world in a fundamental way: things look different from one place to another, and also along the way to and from those places. Doing this activity with mindfulness is tantamount to taking the trip, at least in symbolic terms.

Try this exercise yourself. Moving from one place to another in your home, or from a room of your home to a place outdoors and back again, communicates to your unconscious that you are willing and ready to engage the dream of the journey. By making the effort to physically move in the outside world, you say to the universe and to yourself, "I hear—I accept."

 I have heard the distant call of the journey. In a dream, I have sensed the possibility of personal transformation. Now I open myself to the dream's suggestion and to its promise. I allow the idea of the journey to move in me.

A good traveler is one who does not know where he is going to, and a perfect traveler is one who does not know where he came from.

—Lin Yü-t'ang

Where in the World

The world outside is a big place. The world within is even larger. We heed the call of the voice in the dream of travel. We agree to undertake the journey, wherever the road may lead. Now we wonder where we will go.

The most important feature of this phase of the journey is our willingness to engage the call to travel. Seeds have been presented to us in a dream, and we have planted them. Soon shoots will break forth. We will be on the road and, eventually, gathering the fruit of our labors.

Not having been provided a destination, we reflect on where we will go. We ask ourselves what corner of the world is calling us. Where do we feel drawn? Where is the perfect place... the place the soul will find fulfillment?

The feeling of not knowing our destination is good. We feel a sense of exhilaration about all the possibilities.

"A good traveler has no fixed plans," says the ancient Chinese philosopher Lao-tzu, "and is not intent on arriving."

While we hear and acknowledge his sage counsel, we also know that we live in a world quite different from his—China of the sixth century B.C. Our world is one in which we need to arrange for airline tickets, to reserve hotel rooms, to check the schedules for ferry crossings, to make plans for auto rentals. It may sound hopelessly mundane, but we do live in the here and now—not in some distant romantic past—and we are subject to the conventions of our time.

Still, at this stage in our journey of self-discovery, we have the great luxury to abide in that special emotional territory to which Lao-tzu guides us— the place of having "no fixed plans." Travel, to be truly conscious, should be a process of gathering knowledge about ourselves. Planning too carefully for that can be counterproductive, and even knowing when we have arrived can be limiting.

So we think about where in the world we want to go. We allow ourselves to feel pulled inexorably to a place. We weigh the prospects, consider the alternatives, entertain the possibilities.

Will this be a new place or a place we have visited before?

Will this journey be an opportunity for a totally new experience against the backdrop of a fresh locale, an exotic, unfamiliar geography— or will it be a place that lingers in the memory and to which we always have been drawn to return, this time with new, different eyes and with more seasoned attitudes?

The destination is still shrouded in the clouds, but our journey has begun.

⚭ Set the World Turning ⚭

You hear that unmistakable call to make a journey, but you are not given a destination. What next? There are a number of small things that can help you decide where to go.

These activities are reminiscent of childhood games. Perhaps that is why I like them so much. This phase of travel really is—or should be—childlike. With a strong urge to make a trip, but without a specific place to go, we are like children inventing our own play.

Spin-the-globe is one of my favorite pre-travel exercises. It has to be as old as globes themselves. Simply set the world turning and put a finger down where it stops. That place becomes a possible destination.

Another is flipping at random through a world atlas. Close your eyes, leaf through the pages slowly, and where you stop becomes another potential place to go.

Still another is lazily perusing a travel magazine or a *National Geographic*. Allow the pictures to draw you in. If an image excites you, let your mind drift as far as it will go into that locale. See yourself there, enjoying the sights, savoring the foods, speaking with the people, and delving into its history... and its special mysteries.

The best part of these games is this basic rule: While you do not have to go to these places, you do have to find out one or two facts that you never knew about them. For instance, the mountain range that separates Argentina and Chile is named Tupungato—or in Turkey, one is likely to hear at least six different languages, all of which, together, are called "Turkic"—or in Great Britain, the highest officer of state is neither the monarch nor the prime minister, but the lord high chancellor.

Taking these morsels of information away from pre-travel games can be remarkably helpful as you seek to locate a destination.

Most of the time, your final travel plans have absolutely nothing to do with the exotic lands indicated by your errant fingertip. But the process of physically searching out a place and bringing something back can enhance a journey immeasurably. Wherever you decide to go, these games render the trip a vastly more conscious experience.

I go to where I am called. To discover this destination, I listen deep within. There, in that sacred place, the destination resides. There the journey to self-knowledge is already revealing itself to me.

*I am not born for one corner;
the whole world is my native land.*

—Lucius Annaeus Seneca

The Meaning of the Place

Sometimes we feel the pull of the journey, but we do not know what our destination will be. We go within, we listen, we wait. In time, the map of our journey emerges from the mists.

Other journeys are handed to us fully formed and thoroughly charted. As before, we are beckoned forth by the journey, but this time the summons comes to us from the outside. We are called to a wedding, or a class reunion, or to the bedside of an ailing loved one. Perhaps business takes us to another city, or faraway family members invite us to a holiday gathering.

The destinations of these journeys are already chosen by fate. We know exactly where the trip will take us, but we wonder what will happen along the way, and how we might be transformed by the experience.

All travel is inner travel. Though we did not consciously single out this location, our trip is still very much a journey of self-discovery and personal transformation. Only now we need to discover for ourselves why we might have been called to this particular place over any other.

Since no journey is a mistake, every journey matters.

In the days remaining until we leave home, we ponder the significance of the call to travel, and we try to learn the meaning of the place. If we miss the meaning, we may lose a unique opportunity for growth and self-unfolding.

In a way, we do choose the destination for every journey—but sometimes it appears that we have been drawn to the destination from the outside.

Perhaps we decide on some level of the unconscious that it is time for us to embark upon a journey of self-discovery. What we had believed was a business associate or a family member or a friend is actually our own voice—our deep, unconscious self—drawing us forth to a journey of expanding horizons.

Without full awareness, we have brought about a new journey. We also have chosen the destination.

If this journey had taken place in a dream, what would we have thought the destination meant? We sort through our associations—places where we have been deliriously happy, where danger lurked, where we found someone or lost someone. In a certain place, we learned something vitally important about ourselves; in a particular city or country, we experienced something that forever colors our feeling about it.

All places have meanings for us. This is true whether or not we have been there. We may have direct knowledge of those crooked streets and charming rooftops and serene sunsets. If we do, our meaning for the place will contain those elements—and many more, of course.

A place that is unknown to us still may have some associations, simply because its meaning is universal: Dark Continent, desert island, City of Light, winter wonderland. The Grand Canyon is familiar to anyone—even to people who have never seen it. Likewise Big Ben, the Eiffel Tower, and the Great Wall are familiar to people who have never been to London, Paris, or China.

The challenge for us is to sort out our connections with the place to which we have been called—seemingly by another but really, we know now, by a higher part of our selves.

Exploring the meaning of the place is the key to understanding the journey. When we have learned what the place means for us, we have discovered the way of the traveler.

❀ A New Way of Seeing ❀

What if this were happening in a dream? How would we interpret it?

For several years I had the opportunity of studying the approach to dream analysis developed by C. G. Jung, the great Swiss thinker. Jung's dream world is a realm of myths, archetypes, storybook tales, and fables, all fueled by symbols and their universal or personal meanings.

As I learned more and more about interpreting dreams, I began to apply some of those principles to my waking life. The results were astonishing. When I found a broken window at the back of the house, instead of dismissing it as petty vandalism or the result of a wayward tree branch, I preferred to treat it as I would had it occurred in a dream: as a "breakthrough" in my "outlook." Within days, I enjoyed a tremendous leap of insight about an important aspect of my life.

The "dream" of the broken window—opening for me a new way of seeing—symbolized the insight that would come to me. The event happened in my waking life, but I read it on another level and received a powerful message.

When you travel, whether it is to a place you have chosen for yourself or to a location that has been preordained, ask yourself: If this journey happened in a dream, how would I interpret it?

Write down your destination on a page titled "Meaning of the Place" and make a list of things you associate with that location.

If you do this for every trip you take, your path in life will come more clearly into focus.

The meaning of the place reveals the next step in my soul's journey.
No trip is insignificant. Every time I am given a destination for travel, I am handed an opportunity to learn more about the meaning of my life.

Why to you stay here and live this mean toiling
life when a glorious existence is possible for you?
These same stars twinkle over other fields than these.

—Henry David Thoreau

Into the Unknown

Our journey lies before us like an ancient map of the known world. There is the land we recognize, and the sea, and the rest all around it is a mystery. The cartographers of old called it "terra incognita"—the unknown territory.

We do not undertake the journey lightly.

Deciding to go to a place where we have never been before requires courage. After all, we are literally setting out for our personal "terra incognita." With no knowledge of our destination, we are like those ancient explorers who stared at their dragon-bordered maps and wondered whether it was at all wise to tempt fate.

Even going to a place that we have visited before calls for inner fortitude. We have been there, so we know, generally, what to expect. But new things we might uncover on this particular trip are not known to us.

To leave home in the first place is an act of courage. Many people opt never to do it or to do it as infrequently as possible. We understand that leaving the comforts of where we are and what we know is not easy. Transformation is never easy—and transformation is what the journey promises.

We weigh the pros and cons of leaving home. On the side of staying here is the life we are familiar with—our home, our loved ones, our animal companions, and the simple pleasures of our daily routine.

On the side of leaving home is the possibility of discovery, and with it the thrill of adventure. Journeying, we have the opportunity of finding the answers to questions we have had at home. Going out, we might unearth nuggets of happiness and harmony that have been eluding us in this place.

In spite of our fears, we decide to leave.

We do this with awareness. We know full well that the road is fraught with dangers—that emotional highwaymen may be hiding in the shadows, that dragons of confusion and anxiety may rise up in our path to threaten us. As we navigate our way through the waves, the sea may end abruptly.

No one departs on a journey without some anxiety. Fear of the unknown is an essential part of our human program. If we were perfectly fearless, we could find ourselves in trouble at every turn.

Rational fear is appropriate and can even be a gift. It encourages us to be circumspect—surely one of the qualities that leads to true awareness.

We must not allow irrational fear to take over, however. Fear of that sort can overwhelm us and severely limit the progress of our journey, preventing vitally important lessons from reaching us.

❁ Going with Confidence ❁

Before I undertake any trip, I try to identify my fears—whether rational or irrational—and I consign them to a "Fear Box."

You can do the same. Whenever you begin to feel trip apprehension creeping up behind you, sit down with a pen and paper. At the top, on one side, write "Rational Fears," and on the other side, "Irrational Fears."

Under "Rational Fears" list things that you are concerned about. For one trip, you might write down: I don't know the language—I could be misunderstood or taken advantage of; I can't depend on the quality of tap water for drinking; I don't know where clinics or doctors' offices are in case of an unforeseen health problem.

These are all legitimate concerns, and many of them can be addressed easily before you leave. You can learn a few basic words of the foreign language, so you will not feel helpless at your destination. You can find out ahead of time about water quality and the location of medical facilities by checking guidebooks or making a few simple phone calls.

Under "Irrational Fears," you might jot down something like: I could take the wrong bus and never find the way back to the hotel; I might befriend someone who will then steal my belongings; I'll surely cause a traffic incident because of inexperience driving on the left side of the road.

These are fears for which there is no support in reality. It is absurd, for instance, to believe that taking the wrong bus will make one lost forever. No thief is lying in wait to steal, using the cover of friendship to gain one's confidence. And traffic incidents will depend entirely on driving skills and attention to the rules of the road.

Now here is the interesting part of the exercise. On the sheet of paper, cross out—rather emphatically—all of the irrational fears. They don't exist anymore. Then take each of the legitimate fears and write each one on a separate slip of paper. These go into a "Fear Box."

At last, all your fears about the journey are contained in one place. From time to time before you leave home, open the box and check each fear to see if it is still an appropriate concern. If you handled the matter to your satisfaction, rip the "fear" up and throw it away.

By the time you begin your journey, practically all of your fears will have evaporated.

The road stretches out before me. I know I will encounter obstacles.
The path will sometimes appear circuitous, or worse, perilous.
I have fears.

But still, I go.

*May the road rise with you
and the wind be ever at your back.*

—Irish Toast

The Decision to Go

The gods of travel beckoned us—and we responded.

Now we resolve to undertake the journey.

In the decision to quit this place and go out into the world is the promise of change. Here, in this definitive act of the will, is the seed of our transformation. In spite of our apprehensions, real or imagined, in the face of the unknown, and regardless of the inconveniences, difficulties, and unpredictable demands of the road, we choose to leave all of the comforts of home behind. We decide to go.

We feel a heady rush of excitement from making this courageous decision to act. Nothing will ever be the same, for we have begun the unalterable course to self-discovery.

At the beginning, when we first heard the call to journey in a dream, we wondered at it. Perhaps we were caught off guard and tried to dismiss it.

But the call was too strong—the pull too powerful. The decision to go was still far off, but a restlessness of the spirit had dawned in us.

Fear stopped us in our steps momentarily. We imagined confusions and fierce dragons—emotional, psychological, and spiritual—that might block our way. As we looked closely at each of those fears, however, and saw that they were mostly groundless, they began to shrivel up and disappear. They flew away on the winds of enthusiasm that were sweeping over us.

Now there is only the bright promise of the journey and the doing of it. I have decided to make this journey, we have said to ourselves—and then we have repeated it aloud. We have told our families and our loved ones. In announcing our intention, we have activated the process of going and finding, and of bringing back, the great gift of self-knowledge.

❀ A Travel Shrine ❀

One of the most important ways to work spiritually with a journey is to create a travel shrine.

Your shrine to your journey is an incarnation—a presentation in the outer world of what has been going on inside you since you first dreamed of making a trip. It is a tangible expression of the journey in all its many manifestations, including your excitement, your hesitations, your preparations, and your expectations.

You will find many wonderful uses for the travel shrine, but its primary function is to help you to visualize all the issues that surround your journey. Now, when you have reached the point of decision—when you know that you will be making the journey—this is the time to create your shrine.

Shrines have been with us for untold eons. They stretch far back into antiquity, perhaps to the very dawn of human consciousness. Wherever traces of early civilizations have been uncovered, shrines and altars, prayer panels and sanctuaries have been found.

I begin creating my travel shrine at the moment I hear the first call to journey. I clear a large shelf in my office, lay down a plain white cloth, and install my first honored article—a simple candle. For me, the candle is a symbol of the entire journey, from the period of preparation straight through to my homecoming. More, it represents my willingness to engage the journey. The candle says that I am answering the call of my higher consciousness to fearlessly seek new self-knowledge.

As the days and weeks progress toward my date of departure, I bring more articles of significance to my shrine. If I am going to a place I have never visited, I find pictures of that place and stand them up on my shrine. If I am going to a foreign country, I try to get a few bills or coins of that country's currency and place them on the shrine.

On one journey a few years ago, I was returning to the little town where I grew up. I had been gone from there for almost thirty years and did not know what to expect. Would I even recognize the people and places I knew so well when I was a child growing up there?

My travel shrine for that journey was laden with class pictures from grade school—group photographs featuring a sea of innocent faces surrounding a half-remembered teacher. I placed other mementos on my shrine's altar: a playbill with my name on it; a small sack of marbles; an essay written in pencil, which sported a small gold star; a printed invitation to my eighth grade graduation; a get-well card from a beloved aunt, sent to comfort me when I had the mumps.

By the time I began my journey, which turned out to be remarkably moving and insightful, the candle I had placed there when I started my shrine was surrounded by dozens of other articles of profound meaning.

I left some room on the shrine for what I would bring to it after the trip. When I returned home with new photos of former classmates and teachers, printed invitations to reunion parties, and other fresh mementos, they went onto my travel shrine. Together, all of the articles represented the many facets of that journey.

I make the conscious decision to leave my home and go to another place. I do this willingly and in full expectation that the rewards of self-knowledge will be mine at the end of my travels.

Part Two

THE PREPARATION

Though we travel the world over to find the beautiful,
we must carry it with us or we find it not.

Ralph Waldo Emerson

The spiritual path...
is simply the journey of living our lives.
—Marianne Williamson

Spiritual Provisions

On the road, we are likely to encounter many adventures. To sustain us on the way, to fortify us for our fateful meetings with new people in new places, we will need provisions.

Now it is time to reflect and choose the goods we will want at hand along the road, and to assemble them.

Before the great heroes of mythology left home on their epic quests, they gathered up everything they needed to assure the achievement of their goals. Whether it was to slay a dragon, behead a monster, outsmart an angry goddess, or find the Holy Grail, they wanted to be prepared for the journey. Into their enchanted bags went special potions, three-headed guard dogs, magic ropes, golden arrows, talking seashells, and the rest.

These were the indispensable tools of the trip, without which a hero would not dare to go far from home.

The myths speak in the language of poetry. If a hero sets out with a shield that renders her invincible, we might say that she is protected by superhuman courage. If a hero carries a mirror that induces hypnotism in all who gaze upon it, that might be a metaphor for a mesmerizing charm.

These are more than mere physical necessities for the trip. They are spiritual provisions. As we prepare for our travels, we ask: Does it not make sense to bring along spiritual provisions to meet spiritual challenges and fill spiritual needs? This journey is ultimately an inner journey. We assemble spiritual provisions for this wondrous trek deep into the heart of ourselves— or assist us in conducting our adventure in the world.

Only the appropriate provisions will do. For this journey we must be swift of foot. We stop now and ponder what spiritual impedimenta might serve us and what might be simply unwanted baggage.

Fear not. In this momentous enterprise, we are prompted and guided by our gods of travel.

⚘ Virtues and Values ⚘

I have found it helpful to approach the idea of spiritual provisions for a trip in the most mundane and "non-spiritual" way imaginable. I try to anticipate what I will need in terms of virtues and values, and I simply pack them in with my physical belongings.

You can spiritualize your own travel in the same way.

This is how I happened upon the idea of spiritual provisions. A few years ago, when I found myself traveling several days out of every month, I started the practice of packing with the help of a list. Instead of stuffing my suitcases blindly and hoping for the best, I wrote a list beforehand of all the items of clothing and other things I would need while I was away from home.

After making several successful trips using this method, I began thinking about what else I might need for my journeys. I was not thinking of clothes or shaving equipment or shoe polish, but of something intangible—something I might not be able to see and touch, but that I could sense in another way, and that would be every bit as necessary for my travels as shoes and razors.

That is when I had the idea of packing in with my clothes a simple card that said "Courage."

Some time ago, when I visited family members after a long absence, I packed notes that said "Fortitude" and "Good humor" and "Compassion." As it turned out, I needed every single one of those spiritual attributes during the journey—and they were there for me.

You are the hero of your own journey. Every time you leave home on a trip, you are embarking on a quest for self-knowledge. The spiritual provisions you bring with you are, like that extra sweater in case the weather turns or the swimsuit in the event the hotel has a pool, a kind of insurance for the success of the trip on the spiritual level.

Try this: If you are making a business trip, pack "Bravery" and "Justice" in with your socks, shoes, and toiletries. If you are going off to visit a friend you have not seen for a long time, pack "Kindness" and "Beauty" and "Truth" into the zippered pockets of your suitcase. On a trip to begin a new chapter in your life, take along "Daring."

Here is a short list of some spiritual qualities that might make good provisions for your next journey. Write each word on a separate sheet of high-quality paper, fold, and seal—maybe with sealing wax and your own crest, just to make it official-looking and even more sacred.

Forgiveness	Tactfulness
Charm	Strength
Willingness to Listen	Honesty

Before she left on a recent journey, an artist friend of mine finally got up the courage to pack the one important spiritual provision she had been leaving at home. Quite unexpectedly, during a trip that was supposed to have been a simple private showing for a new client, she met her future husband.

The night before her journey, she had packed away "Love."

In preparing for my journey of self-discovery, I pack spiritual provisions that I will need along the way. The virtues and values I bring give me courage and strength—and are a spiritual blessing to those I encounter on my adventure.

> *There is an expression—walking with beauty.*
> *And I believe that this endless search for*
> *beauty in surroundings, in people, and in one's*
> *personal life, is the headstone of travel.*
>
> —Juliette De Bairacli Levy, *Traveler's Joy*

Goals of the Journey

The goal of our journey is not necessarily the same as the reason we have for making it.

Often, the reason for traveling is given to us beforehand. It is present in the seed of the journey to which we are called: to witness a wedding, to comfort a friend, to conclude an agreement, to attend a reunion. At other times, the reason is more vague—we may simply need a respite from daily routine or crave a change of scene.

But the reason for our journey may not be the same as the goal of our wanderings. Even when we know the reason for travel, we still can choose our own personal goal. And so, we ask, what do we want to accomplish for ourselves on this journey?

When we heard the first faint call to leave home and go off on an adventure, we caught the echo of a goal and a purpose. Since that time, we have searched our heart repeatedly. We wanted to learn why we have been pulled away from home and toward this experience.

Now we are beginning to understand that the primary goal of our journey is to bring something back.

We go out to find and recover that which is missing in our lives.

First and last, the goal of our wanderings is to bring back a higher and richer knowledge of ourselves.

The heroes of old went out to conquer monsters, which we understand represent the ferocious beasts of their own lower natures. They sailed forth to perform Olympian labors, which we take to mean the interior work we do to improve ourselves. They struck out on their bold adventures to bring back the prize, which we know is profound self-knowledge, leading to wisdom.

We are the heroes of our own journey. On our travels, we strive to accomplish our own inner Herculean tasks.

And our goal is that which we understand will bring us closer to what makes us whole. We may aspire to compassion, to generosity, to forgiveness, to love. We may strive for balance, for kindness, for release from false appetites, for acceptance. These make the quest worthwhile and elevate it to the realm of the sacred.

The goals of our journey are ours. We choose them, and we act upon them. And when, on this journey of the heart, we attain them, we complete ourselves.

❦ Bring Awareness ❦

You can accomplish goals on your journey that will enhance your life immeasurably upon your return.

All you need is three small blank cards and a willingness to bring awareness into your travel.

A friend of mine who travels a great deal tells me that he never leaves home without asking himself what he considers the most obvious door-closing question in the world: Why am I doing this?

The first answer he receives is what he considers "the reason for the trip." But he doesn't stop there. He considers the reason for a trip to be quite inconsequential—a simple pretext for getting him away from home and on the road. The more important answer to his question has to do with goals. He rephrases the question to "What do I want this trip to mean for me?"

You can make a journey mean anything at all. If you travel consciously, you will want to make it mean something that will help you learn more about yourself.

Your goals can be general, such as "attaining self-knowledge" or "conquering fear" or "learning compassion." They can also be quite specific. You may want to accomplish "patience" or "self-acceptance" or "a higher appreciation of beauty."

All these goals are attainable.

Remember that you have within you the power to accomplish any goal you set out to attain. To do this, it is necessary to set your goals before the journey as part of your preparation.

As you prepare for a trip, formulate three goals. Keep them simple. They may be: "stop worrying about my appearance," "listen to people more carefully," and "choose food I have never tasted before."

Write these goals out on three-by-five-inch cards and place them on your travel shrine. Then, the night before you leave, tape them side-by-side to the inside of your suitcase. While on the trip, you won't be able to avoid them. You'll look at them every time you need a change of clothes, a new file folder, or your favorite book.

With your goals always before you, you are constantly reminded of your journey's true purpose—to accomplish the key aims you have chosen for yourself.

 My journey is mine. The goals I would accomplish on my journey are mine. I will bring back the Golden Fleece of my own perfected self. The goals I choose direct me to the center of my being. In that secret, sacred place, I dwell serenely, full of the understanding that comes with wisdom.

Go lightly, simply.
Too much seriousness clouds the soul.
Just go, and follow the flowing moment.
Try not to cling to any experience.
The depths of wonder open of themselves.

—Frederick Lehrman

Material Provisions

To make our journey, we also need material provisions.

An empty purse will not get us far along the road. Without money, we cannot progress from one place to another. Without money, we may not be able to return home. Indeed, we may not even be able to leave home.

At least, this is what conventional wisdom tells us.

But we are conscious travelers. We look for a more profound meaning in the notion of material provisions.

Serious advice found in a distinguished nineteenth-century travel book: "Never take a trip you can afford."

How do we reconcile that seemingly paradoxical but seemingly sound counsel against what we know to be the exigencies of travel? For are we not aware that we will need to spend money to purchase fares of passage, to sustain ourselves while we are away, and to provide for our return journey? Even the heroes of mythology needed coins to pay Charon, the ferryman, to take them over the River Styx into the Elysian Fields.

And yet, something compels us to look ever deeper at this puzzle.

At the root of the issue of material provisions is our fear that we will not have enough. Not only enough money, but enough other material supplies—clothes, utensils, books and magazines, even food.

Fear can paralyze us. It can prevent us from taking the next step on the journey. If we remain locked in the fear that we do not have enough, that we will run out, we surely will limit the parameters of our adventure.

When we decide to travel consciously, we spiritualize our journey. All that we assemble of material provisions for the trip must fall under the law of spirit—which is infinite and abundant beyond measure.

We remember the call of the journey.

In the first stirring to travel, the seed was present. And in the seed was all that would be required for the entire arc of the journey—the leaving, the exploring, the returning. Everything necessary to the journey would be provided.

The history of the world's religions show the students of the great masters being sent out to teach people in other lands about the spiritual principles they have learned. Invariably, they are sent out penniless, with "neither rod, nor staff, nor purse." They are on a spiritual mission. On such a mission, spirit will furnish every necessity as it arises.

When we prepare for this journey, we are responding to a call from our higher nature to venture forth and find new knowledge about ourselves. It is a noble quest. We, too, must assume that, under these circumstances, the universe will conspire to assist us.

We attend to our material provisions, of course. We are human. It would be foolish for us to ignore our bodily needs. But we do not dwell on them. We have faith that everything will be supplied—if not as we leave home, then at many points along the path to our destination, and on the same path back.

For we are pilgrims on the road to higher consciousness.

We have answered a sacred call from deep within.

Where we walk, abundance goes before us.

✿ An Abundant Universe ✿

Acknowledging the necessity of material provisions—especially money—is the great reality check of travel.

The challenge in preparing financially at this time is to not allow money, or the lack of it, to limit your journey. You can meet this challenge in a simple and creative way.

I have learned over the years that it is foolhardy to allow extremes to rule here. To deny that you need money and other material provisions for a trip is just as absurd as being overly concerned—sometimes to the point of immobility—about having every single penny in hand before leaving home.

Rather than taking either of those two routes, I have found it useful to confront the issue head-on. You can do this, too.

Take a few dollar bills, or a few bills in the currency of the country to which you are traveling, and a handful of coins, and place them on your travel shrine. For me, this simple act of giving money to the gods of my journey makes a powerful statement. It says, "I am fully aware that I need money to make this trip—and here it is."

If I find that I do not have the money I estimate it will take to make this particular trip, I give money to the shrine anyway. Somehow that seems to prime the pump, and later things work themselves out.

The spiritual principle at work here is this: In an abundant universe, there is always enough. Try to stay in that place mentally, emotionally, and spiritually before, during, and after your trip.

When you work with the issues of your journey on a spiritual level, look for miracles to happen.

 The loving universe, which fosters my self-growth in so many ways, also provides the wherewithal for me to make this journey. As I realize that the journey I am on is a spiritual one, all that I need appears before me.

If "heaven is the Lord's," the earth is the inheritance of man,
and consequently any honest traveler has the right to walk
as he chooses, all over that globe which is his.
—Alexandra David-Neel, *My Journey to Lhasa*

Gifts

In Biblical times, the Three Wise Men packed their saddlebags with gold, frankincense, and myrrh before setting out on their long, arduous journey to Bethlehem.

They were wise, indeed. Gifting is one of the highest purposes of our travel. Giving a gift is the act of offering part of ourselves to another. A gift stays at the new place and allows us, therefore, to stay there in some mystical way.

When we give something to another person, we are making many statements. We are saying, in the first place, that we regard the person as worthy to be receiving something from us. And the gift works in two ways: as a token of esteem for the other and as a symbol of self-esteem for us.

Among the ancients, gift giving was so important that it was ritualized and codified. When an ambassador from the king left his country to visit the ruler of a neighboring kingdom, dazzling gifts were assembled beforehand, then provisions were made for their transportation, and finally for their presentation at court. At every step of the way, prescribed ceremonials were strictly observed.

Temple walls of old Egypt are inscribed with the records of royal visits, during which huge storehouses had to be erected to stockpile the vast number of gifts that had been bestowed upon the crown. Arches and columns in Rome tell stories of imperial visitations that lasted for many weeks—time spans that were necessary to allow for ritual gift giving on a colossal scale.

As we prepare for the journey, we do not forget the gift.

Giving something that is ours will be essential as we progress along the road, when we reach our destination, and on our way back home. We will assemble our gifts now; we will not go forth empty-handed.

When we give, a marvelous and mysterious "dance" is set in motion. Giving makes it possible for the other to return a gift. Although we do not impart gifts for this reason, the pattern of "give and take" is established—the dance has begun.

The dance of gift-giving is karmic in nature. It is rooted in the principle of cause-and-effect. When we give to another, we are giving, in a roundabout way, back to ourselves. This is what Walt Whitman alludes to when he says, "The gift is to the giver, and comes back most to him—it cannot fail . . ."

Like the kings and queens of long ago, we prepare our gifts before the journey. We will give something meaningful, something that will endure.

We give out of our abundance, in gratitude for new friendship, new vistas, and new knowledge. We give because we are thankful for new insights about ourselves—hard won, graciously conferred.

❀ Acts of Generosity ❀

Gathering up a few small gifts is an important part of preparing for your trip. Gifts for people we may meet on the journey need not be expensive—in fact, expensive gifts probably should be avoided—but they should be as personal as possible, and evocative of the place you represent.

Many years ago, traveling in Mexico, I admired a blue scarf that my guide, an archaeology student, was wearing. A moment later, the student had presented the scarf to me as a gift.

This act of generosity astonished me and left me somewhat at a loss for words. Then my traveling companion explained that manners in this culture dictated that some small thing admired by a new friend be given to him as a way to seal the friendship.

For a long time afterwards, I wore the blue scarf. Every time I did, I was reminded of the person who gave it to me—eventually I forgot the guide's name—and that sunny day exploring the ruins of an ancient Mayan settlement.

The scarf has ended up in a trunk that I keep for just such items. I call it my travel treasure chest. When I revisit a place, I open the treasure chest and sift through its contents. A hundred other gifts have joined the scarf now—each of them a tangible, vivid reminder of a particular journey.

But the scarf holds a special place in there because of the lesson it taught me. When I was handed the scarf, I took it gratefully, but I had nothing to give in return. Since then, I never leave home without something to give if the opportunity arises.

Here is a short list of things you might take along with you for gifts: snapshots of yourself, members of your family, animal companions; postcards from your town and your state; small souvenirs from home, like letter openers or tee-shirts; a copy of a favorite book; commemorative or currency coins; a small address book—with your name and address written in as the first entry.

While packing your gifts, remember to make room in your bags to receive gifts from others.

 To give is why I am on this road. In giving, I receive. It is an endless circle of bestowing and accepting. On my journey, I am grateful for everyone who contributes to my further discovery of myself. To honor them, to show my gratitude, I give to others generously, out of the unending abundance of spirit within me.

*Traveling is not just seeing the new; it is also leaving behind.
Not just opening doors; also closing them behind you, never
to return. But the place you have left forever is always
there for you to see whenever you shut your eyes.*

—Jan Myrdal

Closing the Door

Our preparation is ended. We leave home. We close the door.

This final act symbolizes so much—and we do it with full awareness of its importance to the mystic nature of the journey.

The door closes. Behind us now is the life we know so well, with all its comforts and reassuring connections. We leave it—the cozy warm bed, the familiar faces in the pictures on the nightstand, the subtle sounds of the day, the satisfying and consoling scents of this place.

We leave it all.

Around us, like an embrace, home is here in the present, and yet, mysteriously, it is now part of our past. Though we have not yet left home, home seems to have left us. In a peculiar way, we have outgrown it.

We may feel the sadness of leaving descend on us as we stare at the door. Looking at it from this side, the inside, we are still here. When we look at it from the other side—from the outside—we will have gone. This place, home, will be empty. It will exist for us then only in memory.

Closure is essential to the journey. Nothing can happen without it.

In 1519, Hernán Cortés and his party of Spanish adventurers sailed over the Atlantic and arrived on the coast of Mexico. They set anchor in the New World at a town they would name Vera Cruz. For a week they explored the region and heard stories of fabulous empires to the west. Then Cortés sent out a remarkable, harrowing order: burn the ships.

For the soldiers under his command, those proud galleons were like home. More than that, really—for the ships were the only means to take them back to their true homes. Setting torches to them must have taken immense courage, coupled with an unwavering faith in their commander.

But Cortés had prepared them for the order. He had painted a picture of the new, undiscovered lands that lay beyond the mountains and the jungles, awash in riches. To stay behind would be comfortable, of course, but cowardly. To forge ahead would lead them on the road to excitement, fame, and the promise of unimaginable fortunes in gold.

Once they had destroyed their ships—closing the door forever upon a precipitous departure, initiating their journey of discovery—they opened the possibility of glory. In a month's time they would encounter the resplendent Aztec prince, Montezuma. And the history of the western civilization would be changed forever.

We are like those bold explorers. In all of metaphysical literature, gold is the symbol for spiritual riches. To find that gold, we abandon everything we know and march forth from home. We burn our ships.

We close the door.

All travel is inner travel. The end of preparation is the beginning of the journey. We are a step away from the first halting movement toward the thrilling adventure that will end in self-discovery.

We accept the call. We take the step that leads away from home.

We close the door.

✿ Over the Threshold ✿

When you leave on a trip, the last act you perform on the way out of the house—both in a literal and figurative sense—is closing the door.

After many years of travel, I discovered a wonderfully effective spiritual exercise to assure that my trip will be a conscious one. You may want to try it for yourself. It is so simple that it hardly seems like an exercise at all.

I make leaving my house a ceremonial event.

First, I spend some time on the day before I leave thinking about two or three small things I associate with home—things I see and use every day in the house. I usually come up with articles like a favorite coffee mug, a set of keys, a leather bookmark, a pen I keep by the phone for messages.

On the morning of travel day, I take these items and place them on my travel shrine. Symbolically, I am presenting my "comforts of home" to my gods of travel. Here they (and therefore a part of me) will be kept safe all during my journey.

I see this also as an act of blessing. By offering the tokens of home to my shrine, I feel that I am thanking and blessing everything I am leaving behind at home.

Finally, I approach the door. I open it and take my suitcases outside. Now part of me is already on the journey. I am in two worlds.

I come back into the house, position myself at the door, and walk over the threshold, this time with an intense awareness that I am making a crossing. At last, I close the door behind me. I turn and look at the closed door.

Now, truly, I have left home. My journey has begun.

 So long ago, I heard the call of the journey. It beckoned to me in a dream. With all the courage I could muster, I answered the call. Now I close the door forever on the past of myself. I walk into the future. Here, new knowing waits for me; new doors open to me.

Part Three
THE JOURNEY

The months and days are the travelers of eternity.
The years that come and go are also voyagers.
I too for years past have been stirred by the sight of a solitary cloud
drifting with the wind to ceaseless thoughts of roaming.

Matsuo Basho, *The Narrow Road to Oku*

Afoot and light-hearted I take to the open road,
Healthy, free, the world before me,
The long brown path before me leading wherever I choose.
Henceforth I ask not good-fortune, I myself am good-fortune.

—Walt Whitman, "Song of the Open Road"

Getting There

Suddenly, we are on the journey.

It has not truly come suddenly, of course, but only seems so. We have been in preparation for weeks, perhaps months. We have been waiting for this moment since we heard the faint call to journey in a dream, and that may have been a long time ago.

Too often we think the journey will begin when we arrive at our destination. But getting to that destination is also part of the journey. In fact, it may be the most important part. When we turn to our rich cultural heritage of myth, literature, and history, we find that always and everywhere the approach to the destination has been regarded as sacred.

Medieval cathedrals were designed with the concept of the approach foremost in the minds and hearts of the builders. We look at a magnificent cathedral from above, seeing it as a bird sees it: as a cross, with the entrance at the foot and the place of the unfolding mysteries deep inside, at the crossing. From the cathedral's entrance to the crossing is the long walk to the heart of faith . . . the approach.

Ancient civilizations made the processional an indispensable part of every holy ceremony. In the ruins of the forums and markets of the ancient world we discover the remains of wide avenues constructed for the all-important ceremonial approach. Trajan's Column, one of the greatest remnants of Rome's glorious imperial past, is the carved record of one long procession that celebrated the "divine" emperor's life and his contributions to the state.

Mayan, Aztec, and Toltec ceremonial cities in the Americas were planned around processional ways, along which entire populations would move to the place of sacred rites. Egyptian royal mourners marched in solemn procession up long ramps in the Valley of the Kings. Greeks paraded through festooned marketplaces waving banners and palm fronds on their way to temples to honor their gods.

Throughout history, the act of moving in the direction of the destination has been profoundly significant.

So it is for us. We make ourselves aware at every moment that we are moving steadily toward the aim of our journey.

"The journey is its own destination," states an old proverb. All travel on the way to our goal is a consecrated activity.

We know that the process of the journey is itself the journey. Every step we take tells us something more about who we are.

We proceed to our destination.

And as we walk, the procession transforms us.

❧ Magical Steps ❧

Like most of us, I used to travel with only my destination in mind. The last thing that occurred to me was to try to appreciate how I was approaching that destination and to learn what meaning that approach was giving to my travels.

Now, as a conscious traveler, I want to be aware of all the phases of my journey, from the moment I leave my house until the moment I return to it. All the steps between those two points are present with me as I go to where I am going and as I come back.

Here is what I call the "Really" activity. It has helped me to be present in the going and in the coming back. Try it once or twice a day while approaching your destination. You will find that your adventure is vastly enhanced.

Take a moment and close your eyes. Ask yourself two questions: Where am I right now, really? Where am I going, really?

You may be on a plane flying over the Mississippi River. If so, answer yourself with that information. You may be going to a wedding. That is your answer to the second question.

That would be enough to anchor you to the process of the journey. But there is more to this deceptively elementary exercise.

As you rest with these questions and answers, something deeper seems to set in. The word "really" begins to work. You may have the thought that you are on your way to encounter yourself. The wedding, although it is an external event, may symbolize for you the marriage between the parts of yourself, out of which you become an integrated personality. The crossing of the river may rise in your thoughts as an archetypal crossing, like passing over the Rubicon, or the Delaware, or the Red Sea.

This exercise works for all kinds of travel to any destination. You can make your journey a hero's quest if you just ask yourself where you really are right now and where it is that you are really going.

The "Really" activity has never failed to open my eyes to my true destination and to the magical steps that are taking me to it.

I have left my home. I have not yet arrived at the goal of my yearnings. Now I am in the place between places.

My journey, I see, is not only my destination. It resides at every station along the way. And at each stop I have the opportunity to be created anew.

Wherever your journey takes you, there are new gods
waiting there, with divine patience—and laughter.

—Susan M. Watkins

Being Present

At last, we are here.

We have dreamed of this place, and we have prepared ourselves well for coming. Now, with a full, deep breath that is like a long sigh of pleasure and anticipation, we realize that we have arrived.

Challenges arise—not the least of which is the challenge to be present at every moment in this new place. A few seconds ago, it seems, we were at home, and in another few seconds, we will be back there. But now, we are here.

We remember that ancient nomads, moving from one verdant meadow to another, carried their homes on the backs of their pack animals. Where they stopped and pitched their tents was the place they called home.

Long caravans crossing the stretches of Africa and Asia to conduct commerce in faraway lands also took their homes along with them. All of daily life went on as they proceeded from one place to another. Young people fell in love and married. Children were conceived and born. Old people died and were buried. Domestic dramas played themselves out in all their richness. The journey was home, and home was the journey.

When we go out on the journey, we leave home, and yet, in a mysterious way, we take home with us. We may take ourselves away from home, but we do not completely forget about it.

Knowing that, we nevertheless strive with awareness to welcome the next new experience. We do not allow memories of home—or the "home" within us—to intrude upon what may be waiting for us just around the corner in this fresh place.

If our plate is full—full of thoughts of "home"—there will be no room for new and delectable surprises, for the novel tastes and aromas we find in this place. We cannot receive nourishment if we are not open to it.

And so we consciously make room on our plate. We visualize how this place is serving us knowledge about others and about ourselves.

We make ourselves present for this experience.

We understand that all of the pieces of this new puzzle soon will be added to the complete picture of who we are. And where we have been, what we have done, and what we have been in this place far from home, finally, will be a part of what we know as home.

We leave home behind to collect a newer and fuller definition of home.

⚛ Sketching from Life ⚛

You do not have to be an artist to perform this grounding and awareness-engendering activity.

Several years ago, while paging through some eighteenth- and nineteenth-century travel diaries, I was struck by two themes, both having to do with drawing. The first was that the writers of the diaries invariably illustrated their text with little sketches, which were then engraved and included in the published books.

The second theme was that the authors always apologized for their sketches, calling them unprofessional, crude, and amateurish. I appreciated their candor—and remembered that "amateur" comes from the Latin root *amo*, "to love." These small, delicate drawings were made not by trained artists, but by people who loved to travel and who loved to tell other people about where they had been.

Since then, I have been sketching from life while on my trips. I find that it settles me down, anchors me to the place for some time, and, in general, provides some well-needed grounding.

My first attempts at sketching what I was seeing were quite awkward—"amateurish" would be a charitable description. But, to my surprise, the more I sketched, the more I improved.

Taking a cue from those old travel diaries, I concentrated first on trying to illustrate simple architectural details. From my window in a second-floor hotel room in Sienna, I drew what I saw across a narrow alley: a door with an arch over it. I just set down in a sketchbook what I was observing. My finished product showed some of the door but the entire arch, which was the thing that had caught my eye.

On later trips, I found myself drawing other small architectural features: a few spokes of an iron fence in a park, a window shutter, the corner of a terra-cotta tiled roof, a lamppost. Before long, a number of small, thin sketchbooks were accumulating on my travel shelves. Between the covers were verbal and visual memories of my trips, produced by my own hand. I had made myself into a half-decent pictorial chronicler of my travels.

The results of my sketching, however, have been nothing compared to the process. Drawing details of what I am seeing on my journeys gives me a much deeper appreciation of where I am. It affords me the opportunity to be reflective. And it helps me to be fully present at every step, all through a journey.

You, too, will find sketching rewarding. Even tentative, halting attempts at sketching details of what you see on your journey will reap untold rewards.

 Out here, away from home, I draw what I see. Like travelers of old, I lovingly commit to paper the images of my journey. These are reports to myself, sent from new places of my heart. And they are beautiful to behold.

*To awaken quite alone in a strange town is one of the most
pleasant sensations in the world. You are surrounded by
adventure. You have no idea of what is in store for you, but
you will, if you are wise and know the art of travel,
let yourself go on the stream of the unknown.*

—Freya Stark, *Baghdad Sketches*

The Encounter

We are at the heart of the heart of the journey.

To reach this point has not been easy. We have had to summon our
courage and overcome our fears. We have had to prepare thoroughly and
mindfully to arrive here. We have had to leave the warm comforts of home
and surrender to the exigencies of the road.

Now the time has come for the encounter.

The approach to this place has been full of wonder and mystery. Sometimes it has been arduous. But obstacles have departed from our path; vistas
have opened up before us.

We have reached the place toward which we have been moving.

And what do we find here?

When the heroes of mythology went off on their glorious quests, they
equipped themselves with enchanted armor and charms and potions for their

eventual meeting with destiny. These served them along the way, but as all the world's great stories make clear, something more is called for when entering the core of the experience.

At the heart of the journey, every shield and sword, every talisman and incantation, falls away. The hero is left alone and defenseless. This is the most meaningful moment of the journey. It is why the hero undertook the journey in the first place.

Now, as the hero finally reaches the point of encounter, one virtue, above all others, is necessary. That one virtue is valor. Without valor, the hero must abandon the quest—or worse, must submit to the humiliation of defeat. With valor, however, the hero boldly proceeds with the encounter and wins the day.

And so, utterly alone, we offer ourselves completely to this transforming moment.

We take that final step inside the temple.

Now we know.

At the heart of our journey is a person.

Although we did not realize it, this is the person we left home and traveled so many miles to meet. Looking into the face that looms before us, we know suddenly that we were destined for this encounter at this time—in this place.

This person is like us in many ways and in other ways is quite dissimilar. The eyes that gaze into our eyes are faintly familiar—but decidedly foreign. The hair, the features, remind us of hair and features we have known—and yet are somehow different, vaguely exotic.

A smile breaks on the face of the person we are beholding. We feel accepted and included. We feel embraced. Our heart opens.

For a moment we believe that we have done nothing to earn this gracious welcome. Then the thought sweeps over us in sudden understanding, like a strong wind from the corridors of the temple: with valor we have come to this moment in time; with courage we have accepted the call of the journey. We have earned this prize.

Our prize is to embrace and to be embraced by the stranger.

The stranger standing before us has qualities that we have been lacking. The stranger seems to know more, to see more, to feel more, to have many more dimensions. Beauty, serenity, compassion, and wisdom emanate like a golden aura from the stranger.

We have glimpsed this stranger through windows that opened briefly in our quiet times. Now, our senses are filled with the presence of this new person. In a flush of emotion, we feel complete.

We recognize the person. This is not a stranger at all.

We understand

The stranger and I are one.

The stranger is me, transformed.

❧ Reflections of Who You Are ❧

At the center of every journey are people. At first they may appear to you as strangers. But really they are reflections of who you are.

People you encounter on your journey are mirrors of yourself. Describing them is an excellent way to learn more about you—not just the "you" you have known, but also the "you" into which you are transforming.

On a trip, you might encounter dozens of people. Choose one or two of them—people who stand out in your mind—and write down some of the things that strike you about them: kind, a bit of a temper, wonderful laugh, serious, careful with words, entertaining, honest. Because the person you are describing is your mirror, these attributes are also yours.

This little exercise is simple, but its rewards are tremendous. It gives us the opportunity to see ourselves externalized and to appreciate ourselves more than we ever have.

The stranger at the heart of my journey is me—transformed. I have come all this way to find this new person.

At the center of my wanderings, the world is strange, wonderful, and new. All that I see and touch now is new.

With a rush of recognition, I lovingly accept and embrace my new self.

Travel is more than the seeing of sights; it is a change
that goes on, deep and permanent, in the ideas of living.

—Miriam Beard

Gifting

We have recognized ourselves in the stranger. Now we move to take what
we first saw as foreign in the stranger and to make these things part of the
familiar.

When we incorporate the truths we have just discovered, we transform
ourselves. We are renewed.

But how do we accomplish this? We want somehow to merge with the
new experiences in order to make them truly ours. If we do not, if we are un-
touched by what is all around us, we will remain the person we were when we
began our journey.

To bring about the union of the familiar and the new, unfamiliar parts of
ourselves, there must be an exchange—a giving and a receiving. We offer to
another a token of the self we knew so well—the part of us that left home
and courageously embarked upon this journey of self-discovery.

We receive from the other the new part of ourselves.

Ceremonial gift giving among the ancients, at the state level, was ritually prescribed and incredibly extravagant. Stories of these exchanges have come to us in great detail through written and pictorial history. Mutual presentations of exotic offerings between rulers of fabled kingdoms went on for days and weeks.

When the Queen of Sheba visited King Solomon in Judea in 950 B.C., long caravans of riches and huge herds of domesticated beasts followed her. When Queen Cleopatra entered Rome in 46 B.C., more than five hundred royal barges laden with the dazzling wealth of Egypt preceded her up the Tiber, pulled by hundreds of oxen.

For our ancestors, behind the grand gesture of giving and receiving lay the concept of honoring the new and unfamiliar, and paying generous tribute to it, in order to somehow merge with it. This large-scale symbolic mingling of kingdoms was designed to elevate both the giver and the receiver.

In fairy tales, the hero, upon his victorious return from his quest, is greeted by the king and awarded the hand of the princess and half the kingdom. We understand these as metaphors for union on a new and higher level, incorporating both the old and the new in one.

In the giving of gifts brought from home, we offer ourselves the possibility of personal transformation. By the same generous act, we offer the recipient of our gifts the same opportunity for personal growth.

To the other, our gift is foreign, strange, and exotic.

To us, what we may receive in return is likewise novel and unusual. Even if no token is offered us, the person we encounter may be our gift.

The hand of the princess, half the kingdom—in the merging of ourselves with the foreign, we become new.

❀ A Token of Your Esteem ❀

You brought gifts from home along with you on your trip. Now is the time to give them.

Some of us go on journeys with presents but forget to hand them out—or wait for what we think might be a more appropriate time. I used to return home with gifts I had spent time and effort assembling before a trip but ended up never distributing at my destination.

When do you give a gift? Not only when, but also to whom, and how? These are good questions to ask yourself now, as you pull from your suitcase the snapshots of yourself and loved ones, and other small reminders of the place you call home.

In matters of gift giving, I have learned that the heart knows better than the head. There is something false in trying to rationally decide who will receive your gift or when you should give it. The heart seems to know the answer to those questions. My advice is to go with your heart.

A little courage may be necessary here. You may be shy, or just a bit reserved. If so, you are not in the habit of reaching out to new people, especially with your heart.

But you have undertaken this trip with courage; you have come boldly here, to the heart of your journey. Surely you can offer a simple gift to a new acquaintance.

See yourself offering your gift from home—a token of your esteem for the receiver. See the person accepting it graciously, regarding it with respect and gratitude.

Remember that in giving a small gift to someone new, you are doing what you came here to do. The "new person" is a mirror of yourself. You are completing your journey of self-discovery.

Giving of myself is a surrender of the past. Accepting the new is why I have made this glorious journey.

I take one step away from myself, and I am in a new world.

But no, this is the same world: I am new.

Travel broadens perspectives and teaches new ways to measure quality of life. Many travelers toss aside their hometown blinders. Their prized souvenirs are the strands of different cultures they decide to knit into their own character.
—Rick Steves, *Europe Through the Back Door*

Collecting Mementos

Even in this blissful moment of encounter and exchange, our minds race ahead and race back.

Both ahead of us and behind us is home.

We are at the midpoint of the journey. From here, we start back again. And so our thoughts are of home: the home we came from, which carries our past identity, and the home we are going back to, which will be changed because we are changed.

While the fire at the center of this experience still burns brightly, we are drawn to look for something to take away from here. The prospect of returning home empty-handed is unthinkable. We need to recover a tangible reminder of this place.

We search for the mementos that will recall this enchanted time long into the future.

When Christopher Columbus returned from his first voyage of discovery in the New World, he brought back to his patron, Queen Isabella of Spain, "the treasures of the Indies"—gold and other precious minerals, parrots, exotic animals, wood, maize, sweet potatoes, plantains, and pineapples. If anyone doubted that Columbus had found an entirely new land, here was proof positive.

Each gift he presented at court carried the scent of its place of origin. These mementos were pieces of the great mosaic of world discovery. For Columbus, they were a remembrance of the fascinating lands he had so recently trod; for Isabella, they were the distilled essence of the lands themselves.

History records that in the year following the first triumphal homecoming of Columbus, court doctors in Spain used an assortment of peppers brought back from the New World, unknown in Europe at that time, to treat an ailing Isabella. Symbolically, "the new" was used to regenerate "the old"— and a memento from the epic journey was the medium of the healing.

We search for a tangible remembrance of this place—a relic from here that will have a special meaning for us. We look for something that epitomizes the stage upon which we have acted out our transformation.

This search for something of value to our heart is a quest-within-a-quest. It is the journey in microcosm.

Seeking the perfect memento, finding it, bringing it back—this is the very essence of the journey. We undertake it with care, with awareness.

The prized souvenir we pack away to bring back is incontrovertible proof that we have discovered our own New World.

✿ A Recollection of the Journey ✿

I used to regard souvenirs as a necessary bother. They were part of the unavoidable obligations of travel. Most of the time I thought of them at the last minute—usually as presents for family and friends back at home.

Lately, though, I have been seeing the wisdom of choosing appropriate mementos of a journey. Now they have become for me reminders of where I have been—both in the literal and the figurative sense.

You will find that selecting and taking back mementos will add immeasurably to the experience of your journey.

Every small memento from a trip is a recollection of the journey in tangible form. At the time you buy a souvenir, or are given a token of remembrance, it may seem insignificant. Once you are home, however, the small item will expand into something much larger in your mind and your heart.

Since everyone has a different experience of a journey, everyone will take away from that experience something entirely different. The things you are given on a trip or buy to take back home will be completely unlike anyone else's remembrances. That is what makes them so special.

You will want to look for something that has a powerful meaning for you—something that will recall a transformative aspect of the trip. It may be something as simple as the menu from a café where you met someone who has become important for you. Or it could be a pass to a museum or a performance where you received a significant insight.

Forget buying something expensive. I have never found the most important mementos to have anything to do with cost. They are not for impressing people back home with a fancy price tag. They are for making you aware of the journey as an inner experience.

Choosing mementos in this way, you may even come up with souvenirs that you had thought trite—a paperweight of the Empire State Building or a glass snow-globe of the Eiffel Tower. What might be a cliché in another context might be just the right memento for you to take back home.

You will find that the simplest things will create an enormous impact upon your return.

I collect evidence of my travels. When I end this journey, I will have these things to remind me that I was courageous—that I did not shrink from change. These tokens are the proof of my transformation.

Now I am ready to return from whence I came.

Part Four

THE HOMECOMING

He who returns from a journey is not the same as he who left.

Chinese Proverb

We leave behind a bit of ourselves
Wherever we have been.

—Edmond Haraucourt, *Choix de Poésies*

Leaving for Home

Getting to this place required much effort; adapting to it took courage and patience. Now we don't want to leave.

The pain of separation is much like what we experienced as we left home. In a strange way, this place has become home.

And now we feel the stirrings of other apprehensions. Questions begin to occupy our thoughts: What will life be like away from here? What will we find when we go home?

The poet says that we die a little when we leave a place. And so it is.

The prelude to homecoming involves completing and concluding all that this place has meant to us. While we draw all the strands of this place together, we reflect on the fabric of our traveling, a perfect tapestry, which we are weaving with our many experiences. We are seeing the end of things here. We are sensing fullness and consummation.

The arc of our journey now begins to descend, like the sun passing mid-day. In the golden light of our last moments here, we recollect and we imagine our next steps into the future.

Finding the way back home from a quest is a common theme in all great literature. Getting back from the place that once was our destination is as important as getting to it—and just as filled with meaning for us.

When Theseus was about to enter the Labyrinth to hunt down and slay the dreaded Minotaur, he agonized over how he would find his way out of the maze. His lover, the beautiful Ariadne, came to his assistance with a ball of thread. She told him to tie one end of it to the cave's entrance and unwind it as he went through the tortuous passages. In this way he would be able to retrace his steps to home.

Theseus was successful in his quest; he killed the monster, and, using Ariadne's thread, returned home to tell the tale.

Other heroes have not been so fortunate. Orpheus, when he left the Underworld, disobeyed the gods by looking behind him to see if his beloved Eurydice was following him. The moment he turned to look, Eurydice was drawn back into the darkness of Hades forever.

Two lessons arise from the myths. We see that finding our way back home is significant. And we learn that once we depart we are not to look back.

Ariadne's thread, the theme of our journey, is our lifeline home. To return safely from this place, we must be aware of why we came here and what we accomplished. The thread that runs throughout this trip must be acknowledged. Our conscious leaving will assure that we go home triumphant and fully satisfied.

The admonition the gods gave to Orpheus rings in our imagination: "Do not look back." We are to close this chapter of the journey and close it firmly. To wonder whether we truly completed all we came here to do, to imagine for a moment that we have left the journey somehow undone, would show a lack of faith in our gods of travel.

Memories—oh, yes. We will be looking back in that way when, home at last, we sort through the treasures of the place we have been.

We depart now, with respect, affection, and gratitude, laden with our experiences of self-discovery.

We depart.

❦ Reflecting on the Place ❦

With a few homemade ceremonies, you can make your departure one of the most important phases of your journey.

Often you are not even given the opportunity to reflect on the place you are leaving or on the wonderful things that happened there. In the commotion of packing, arranging transportation, and attending to other details, you might forget a ritual that can put the entire journey into perspective.

On the day before my departure, I always leave two or three hours to be by myself. Alone, I feel the pangs of leaving and the swelling of gratitude for having been here. Awash in these feelings, I perform three ceremonies.

I pass these on to you.

First, revisit two or three specific locations that have become important to you—an outdoor café where you had coffee every morning, a bridge where you watched sailboats float lazily by, an isolated stretch of beach. Consciously say good-bye. If you are alone, you can say good-bye aloud and thank the place.

Second, choose one of the locations and write a simple good-bye note to it (and, by extension, to all your locations): "Farewell—and thank you!" Leave the note there.

Finally, as you leave the place where you have been staying, bless it for the next person. You have the power to bless—and this is one of the best ways to use it.

I depart this place that has given me so much. I express my affection and my gratitude for the insights it has provided me.

Before I go, perhaps never to return, I leave my blessing. May all who come here be healed in the discovery of their true selves.

Only that traveling is good which reveals to me the value of home and enables me to enjoy it better.

—Henry David Thoreau, *Journal*

The Return

We are home!

We return with a full heart. We come home carrying with us the prize from the quest, the promise of a bright future.

While on the journey, from time to time we revisited this place in our mind. During a lull in our adventures, we wandered back here and, in our imagination, walked among these rooms, so filled with meaning, so imbued with our spirit.

Now we are back, and what we left behind glows brighter, greets us, and welcomes us. We went forth from this place with hope. We return to it with a treasure trove of experiences and with a new knowledge of ourselves.

This new knowledge continues to unfold.

While out in the world, away from here, we have not been idle. We have successfully met the challenges presented by new places and new people.

These encounters have made us stronger and wiser.

We return joyful, energetic, prepared to accept new ways of seeing others—and ourselves.

This, the return home, is also part of the journey. Making our way back mindfully connects us with the universal idea of homecoming.

In ancient Rome, when generals returned home from a victorious campaign, they camped outside the city for days, sometimes weeks, as a grand entrance was planned and a triumphal arch was constructed. Finally, after prodigious and meticulous preparation, they began the parade into the heart of Rome. Long carts filled with the spoils of war, with exotic animals, with captive enemy officers, preceded the conquering general, who rode in a golden chariot drawn by white steeds.

Those glorious entries into the forum became the stuff of legend, celebrated in historical accounts and still visible on the carved columns and temple walls of modern Rome.

We also return triumphant, with new self-knowledge born in other places.

Another universal idea emerges: putting the household back in order. What we find upon our arrival may not be the same place that we left. If the order of the home is the metaphor for the way we were before we embarked on the journey, then some modifications may be necessary—for we ourselves have changed in the time we were away.

Ulysses comes home to Ithaca after a twenty-year absence—ten of it spent in mortal combat in Troy and another ten engaged in amazing adventures on the long voyage back. His kingdom is in disarray. His estates are in ruin, his lands are lying fallow, and his beloved wife is being courted by a score of brutish suitors.

Quickly, with the strength and wisdom gained on his epic journey, he rids the kingdom of the encroachers and decrees the restoration of his houses and the planting of his fields.

Now, truly, he is home.

And so we return. We reenter our home in triumph. We set everything in order.

Slowly, as we rest in this new place, which is the old place transformed, we feel the immensity of what we have undertaken and accomplished, and we are warmed at this familiar, embracing hearth.

❀ Your Triumphal Arch ❀

I never paid much attention to entering my house when I returned from a trip. Coming home was about getting in the door, putting my bags down, and sinking into an easy chair.

But lately I have made much more of my return—and it has served to make my entire journey a richer, more conscious experience.

You, too, can make a ritual entrance into your home.

When you left on your trip, the last act you performed on the way out of the house—both in a literal and figurative sense—was closing the door. You may have made a little ceremony of it by closing the door behind you slowly and with awareness of your leave-taking.

Coming home presents the opportunity for doing the same, but in reverse. Before entering the house, stand outside for a moment, remember that you are still "away from home," then open the door and step inside.

Crossing the threshold is an act of momentous importance. A moment ago you were still on the road, still a traveler. Now, in the next moment, you are across the line, back home. The doorway is your triumphal arch.

You close the door behind you with the same intense clarity that accompanied you when you left on your trip. You are inside.

You are home.

If you listen carefully—before you survey the rooms, before you open your mail, before you check the messages on your phone and on your computer—you will hear the cheering of the crowds as you enter your domain in triumph.

 In the land of the stranger I encountered the monsters of self-doubt, fear, and limitation. I met them on the field and won the day. Now I return triumphantly in a chariot of gold.

I enter the city of my birth crowned with laurel. I am home.

*If we are always arriving and departing, it is also true
that we are eternally anchored. One's destination is never
a place, but rather a new way of looking at things.*

—Henry Miller, *Big Sur and the Oranges of Hieronymus Bosch*

To Honor the Adventure

We have come home.

It is cause for celebration!

But for just this short period of time, we remain quiet and reflective. Our celebration is an interior one—no less joyous than an outward observance with family and loved ones. Now we crave stillness to process where we have been and what we have done—to honor the adventure.

Later we will announce our homecoming. We will reveal ourselves to the people in our lives. We will show them what we have brought back from our travels. At this moment, however, we are alone, assimilating our experiences and basking in the accomplishment of the journey.

Slowly, we make a much smaller excursion   this one around the very home that we left. We visit the four corners of this world, one by one. It has diminished in size somewhat. It is smaller than we remembered.

Or have we somehow gotten larger?

They are still here, these things we left behind. An article of clothing, eliminated from the packing process, lies on the bed. A half-cup of coffee sits on the counter. And, on the table, spread open to a favorite section, is the morning newspaper of the day we embarked on our journey.

Suddenly we begin to see everything around us in a new way.

All of this represents the old. But we are not the same as we were when we last handled these things. We have been transformed by the journey. We have encountered "the other"—our mirror image—and that meeting has made us stronger, wiser, and more whole.

The hero enters the city in triumph, and all that was left behind at home is charged with the new radiance of personal transformation.

We come home, having braved the world away from here, bringing back the knowledge of self that will make our lives fuller and more compassionate.

We acknowledge and honor the old—all that was here when we left home. And we welcome in the new.

All of it is good.

For we realize that nothing we see, nothing we hear or feel, has a meaning beyond us. All simply is. Our conscious awareness bestows definition to everything in our world.

Alone, we wander through this microcosm of our universe, accustoming ourselves to it again.

The adventure of exploration and discovery has almost reached its glorious conclusion. Tomorrow we will tie all the ends of this amazing tapestry together. Today we sit quietly, still weaving those threads, regarding with wonder all that has been altered—upward—by our journey.

🐚 Offerings 🐚

One of the most glorious moments in your journey comes when you have arrived home, entered the house, and closed the door behind you.

Your trip is over, but your journey is not.

You can give this moment a spiritual meaning with a simple ritual that goes back in antiquity to the epic travelers of history and myth. This is a an extraordinary time—and savoring it and celebrating it will add to the closure of your trip.

A few years ago, after I began making travel shrines for each of my journeys, I stumbled upon a little ceremony that I now perform as an indispensable part of my return home.

If you read the great stories of world literature, you see that heroes, on their return from a great quest, often make their first visit to the temple of the god or goddess who protected them through their journey. Symbolically, they acknowledge divine assistance in undertaking and completing their adventures.

They approach the temple altar, say a few words of thanksgiving, and place upon it a libation of wine and a dish of delicacies—figs, dates, nuts, and other treats. Offering these tokens to the deities is the hero's way of paying tribute to the powerful spiritual forces that guided him on the road, and brought him back safely home.

I perform the same ceremony at my travel shrine—and I do it literally. I pour out a small bowl of wine, prepare a dish of sweets, and place them on my altar. These living items—representing not only sustenance, but also opulence—sitting there among the other emblems and mementos of my journey, lend a vital new energy to the entire shrine.

When you offer your token delicacies to the gods of your shrine—whether they are the wine and dried fruits of the ancients or your own modern counterpart—remember to sing out your hero's jubilant song: "I celebrate the new . . . I honor the old . . . Give thanks for the end of the journey!"

At the altar of my epic journey, I offer gratitude to the powers that have impelled me to self-discovery. For me, as for the heroes of old, the journey draws to a close in thanksgiving. In the temple of this journey to the heart of myself, I bask in the light of new wisdom so dearly won, so graciously given.

*Once you have traveled, the voyage never ends, but is
played out over and over again in the quietest chambers.
The mind can never break off from the journey.*

—Pat Conroy

The New Order of Things

Now, to adjust to what we have found upon our return.

Things are different. No, things are the same—we are different. We
notice subtle changes, quiet shifts of energy. At home, we seem to see more;
at work, we undertake old tasks with more detachment.

The journey has brought about a new order of things.

We are no longer the same people we were when we left home. Finding
who we are now, and arranging everything in our world around that new definition, is our challenge.

In fairy tales, the main character often undergoes a profound change at
the end of an adventure. A frog is turned into a knight. A pauper reveals himself to be a prince

Before life can be lived "happily ever after," a fundamental change must
take place.

Ovid's *Metamorphoses* takes its name from the poet's stories of change. In one, the sculptor Pygmalion falls in love with his own creation, a life-sized statue of a beautiful woman. From Mt. Olympus, Venus takes pity on the artist and transforms the statue into a living woman, Galatea.

In another of Ovid's stories, the beautiful Daphne, fleeing the advances of the god Apollo, runs for help to her father, a river deity. When she reaches the bank of the river, her father hears her plea, and she is changed into a laurel tree—which forever afterward is sacred to the worship of Apollo.

Personal transformation is a theme throughout world literature. People are turned into pillars of salt as punishment; they become trees, birds, and flowers as rewards for good deeds. Always, the change is a lesson.

We, too, are transformed by our recent experiences away from home. Now, as a new routine begins to emerge in our daily life, we start to see the many sides of our personal metamorphosis. And it delights us.

The change that has come upon us is growth.

Everything in our world now needs to be evaluated to see whether it fits with the new person we have become. This is a time of observing, analyzing, weighing, and imagining alternatives.

Perhaps the greatest gift of the journey is the awareness that we have the power to re-create our lives. Such is the magic of travel! We have been changed by our experiences on the journey. Now, the legacy of the journey is the power to assume an active role in our growth.

Travel transformed us; now we transform ourselves.

We do it by instituting a new order in our world. The new world around us conforms to who we truly are now.

A Taoist saying tells us, "The journey is the reward."

Suddenly, we comprehend all that is being said in these rich words of wisdom. The gift of the journey is nothing less than a new world of our own creating.

❧ The Power to Transform ❧

You can do something simple and symbolic to lock in your acknowledgment that everything has changed—and that you have the power to transform your world.

Now that you are back from your journey, you can refashion everything around you. The truth is, you not only have the ability to change things, but you also have the obligation to do so.

Some people, when this realization sweeps over them, reorganize their lives in ways they never would have imagined before leaving on a trip. I have seen friends do everything from rearranging the living room furniture to quitting a boring job. Travel had an impact on them that remained after they returned home and impelled them to take some transformational action.

You do not have to go as far as getting into a new line of work to change things in your world after a journey—although that certainly may be an option. Most people find that they return to both home and work with so many fresh ideas and novel approaches that life may seem to be entirely new.

Here is a small but effective activity that will signal your power to create a new order of things. Find something that you used almost every day before your journey—a favorite coffee mug, an article of clothing, a familiar piece of recorded music, a particular scented soap.

Take this symbol of the "old order" of your life, put it away in a closet, and replace it with a new version—preferably something you may have brought back with you from your travels.

This small, conscious re-creation of a part of your world registers on the unconscious as a powerful act of self-transformation. Other, larger changes will follow.

 The journey has given me the power to change my world.
I take that power in my hands and, like the magician that I am, transform everything around me. In this way, I make my world conform to the new person that is my discovered self.

And the end of all our exploring
Will be to arrive where we started
And know the place for the first time.

—T. S. Eliot, "Little Gidding"

Completing the Circle of the Journey

We close the circle of travel that began so long ago with our leave-taking. We know that marking the end of travel is as important as acknowledging the start of it.

With awareness, we draw the circle up.

Now is the time for reviewing and planning. This is the moment of insight—of hindsight and foresight.

The angel of the journey spoke to us in a dream, saying, "Go forth." We heard the distant call of travel and entertained the possibility of change. To leave home and venture out on the road would take courage, which we summoned toward the promise of a significant encounter.

Flush with anticipation, we closed the door upon the past. We brought with us fortitude, patience, perseverance, valor—our spiritual provisions.

The path to the destination was not easy—setting out in the great unknown never is easy. Thorns of discord were strewn about on the road; unexpected emotional ruts pitted the trail. And sometimes fear haunted us.

At last we arrived at the new place.

Shakespeare tells us that "journeys end in lovers meeting." This journey culminated in an encounter that changed us to our very heart. Truly, lovers met. We have seen ourselves in the mirror of the other, and we have been transmuted at the sight.

Leaving the new land was as difficult as leaving home had been. In a strange, mystical way, that place had become home—for, indeed, it was "home" to the emerging of our new self.

We gathered up mementos—relics of the journey. These precious, mute objects would tell the tale.

And suddenly, perhaps all too soon, we were finding our way back along the road toward home. Again the path was uneven and arduous. But this time we had the advantage of familiarity, and the thread of the journey— its special theme—to guide and comfort us.

"Where we love is home," says the poet Oliver Wendell Holmes in "Homesick for Heaven." "Home that our feet may leave, but not our heart."

We walk from room to room in this place that is as well known to us as the contours of our own face. Here is where we lately spent so much time, laughed with family and friends, loved, wept, celebrated, pondered, and planned our life. It is rich with the shadows of our comings and goings.

But we have changed. Now we alter this environment, which is the abode of "the old," to fit the new person we have become. We re-create our world, as we have re-created ourselves. And thus we bring the journey to a close.

The covenant we made with our angel of travel in those days long ago is now fulfilled.

We rest in the satisfaction of having found the courage required for this adventure. All around, this new world of our own making comforts us.

In the silence, the Voice comes to us: Every journey is a journey inward. Travel in the outer world is a metaphor for the inner journey.

And the end of the journey is transformation.

❀ A Sacred Event ❀

If you created a shrine to your journey, now is the time to dismantle it. Do it with a sense of ceremony, and you will elevate the conclusion of your trip to a sacred event.

Even if you did not create a travel shrine, you can make a ritual of putting away the things you have brought back with you.

Journey's end is a time for reflection and celebration. Closure is one of the most important aspects of a trip. Leaving a journey open-ended is tantamount to not completing a delicious meal or not finishing a really good book. Ending a trip properly brings enormous satisfaction.

The literature of travel is full of references to the ends of journeys: the leprechaun finally finds the pot of gold at the end of the rainbow (a metaphor for the arc of the journey of life); lovers finally kiss at the end of the movie (a symbol for transformation in union).

By the end of a trip, your travel shrine has accumulated an assortment of meaningful objects. It holds pre-trip tokens such as travel brochures, itineraries, and pictures of family, friends, and animal companions, which you left here for symbolic safekeeping while you traveled. In with those are post-trip souvenirs such as ticket stubs, menus, postcards, trinkets, snapshots, and small rocks or pieces of driftwood.

Your shrine also holds your "Fear Box"—that little box into which you placed only your rational fears before you left home.

The first part of the "ceremony": Take the little slips of paper that contain your fears and burn them. Send the ashes to the winds.

Next, put away almost all of the keepsakes on your altar or your travel shrine. Hold back one or two things to remind you of the journey, and place them where you will see them every day.

Finally, lovingly, take the shrine down.

My journey is over, but my discovery of myself is only beginning. I am at peace.

Part Five

RECOUNTING THE TALE

The hero of my tale,
whom I love with all the power of my soul,
whom I have tried to portray in all his beauty,
who has been, is, and will be beautiful, is Truth.

Leo Tolstoy

I may not have gone where I intended to go,
but I think I have ended up where I intended to be.

—Douglas Adams

Assembling the Threads of the Journey

As a new routine at home and at work begins to set in, we ask, What has happened? Where have we been?

Something wonderful has happened. We have been on a journey of exploration and discovery that has led us back to the heart of ourselves.

Now, in the comforts of home, in the warmth of the blazing hearth, we prepare to tell the tale of our wanderings. This has been our own epic expedition, and it has been filled with amazing adventures.

We gather the errant corners of our story.

It may be that someone who hears our tale will decide upon a change of course by the example of our experience. Perhaps a prospective voyager will be able to avoid the pitfalls to which we nearly succumbed. Someone seated around the fire with us will be inspired to make a similarly brave journey.

Our tale will be like a flint that ignites the hearts of those who hear it.

The stories of the great adventures are our teachers. Heroes set off on demanding quests, perform miraculous tasks with divine assistance, and return home victorious. At the end of the journey they reap the rewards.

We understand that these epic tales are metaphors for the upward movements of consciousness. We step into the winged sandals of the hero.

Like the hero, we started out, we accomplished, we returned. Now we are finding the thread that runs throughout and ties the tale together.

Our story is valuable, for it is the record of our self-exploration and self-discovery. And so we formulate the arc of our personal narrative. Others may find in it a route to their own salvation.

An inscription was scratched on one of the caravels of Columbus, 1492: "Following the sun, we left the old world."

Thus begins our own story.

And now we relive the chronicle, review it, and set it out. We followed the sun; we left the old world. What we found in the new world, and how we made our way back, is the stuff of our epic tale.

❀ Your Epic Tale ❀

You may have been keeping a "feelings journal" on this trip. This kind of writing is a record of how you felt and what was happening to you while you were traveling.

Now you may want to write something entirely different: the story of your trip as you lived it—not from the inside, as it were, but from the outside, as if you were the major character in your drama.

I stumbled upon this exercise after a trip I took with some friends and their eleven-year-old daughter. I heard the girl telling the story of her journey to one of her classmates. She treated it exactly like a fairy tale—with herself as the beautiful princess.

Since then I have returned again and again to this activity as a way of elevating my travel to the level of myth.

Writing your tale is a good way to assemble the threads of the journey. And, although easy, it is one of the most important activities you can do at this stage to heighten your trip's spiritual content.

Start with a simple list of what actually happened while you were away from home. Find a quiet time. Sit down with pen and paper. Then, in chronological order as you remember them, write out a list of things that you did or that happened to you on the trip. Try not to judge your items ("I went to that museum but probably shouldn't have..."); just jot down the facts.

When you have finished, you should have a good chronology. Now organize your list into a narrative story. Be sure to put everything into the past tense and to refer to yourself in the third person ("She did such-and-such... he said such-and-such.")

After your story is complete, two things remain to be committed to paper. At the top of the page, write out the words, "Once upon a time ... " and at the end write, " ... lived happily ever after."

The story of your journey has now become an epic legend.

When you see the tale of your trip written out in this way, you will begin to understand it in the context of an archetype. Objectifying your experience has a way of making your personal experience seem universal. And, to be sure, it is.

We are the heroes of our own story. We deserve an epic tale to document our exploits.

 My story is the journey of my life through time and space. It is a tale of valiant undertakings—fording rushing rivers, making my way through the dark woods, crossing the long, wide fields, battling dragons—this leads me to the crystal palace of wisdom.

Returned, I gather the threads of the journey. I prepare to tell my tale. And what I have to say is this: "Once upon a time ... "

You will bring back pots and pictures. A sheaf of photographs.
A jingle of coins. But you will bring back more.
A vision of a wide world. Remembered laughter.
New friends. New understanding.

—Pam Brown

Displaying the Treasures

The time has come to share the treasures from our epic adventure.

All the days of the journey have led to this moment.

When we returned home, we were silent. We sat and pondered where we had been, what we had done. Events along the road were awesome, filled with wonder. Slowly, the arc of the journey began to emerge.

As the threads of the tale appeared, one by one, we gathered them and pulled them in. In time, they would come together to make the fabric of our re-created self.

We encountered the scribe within. With quill in hand, we set down our tale. As we did, the spirits of those far-off places rose up. A story glowed through. What seemed like random experiences are now, we see, part of something whole. Each action contributed to another to make something full and rich.

The chronicle of the journey is a story on a grand, universal scale. It carries profound meaning not only for us, but also for everyone who is called by the gods of travel to venture forth from home.

Virgil, the celebrated court poet, stands in the midst of the banquet hall. He makes his way among the revelers reclined upon their couches, through a throng of servants hauling heaps of delicacies brought in from the far reaches of the Empire. He approaches the long tables where the imperial family is assembled. His eyes meet the eyes of the Emperor. It is as if he will declaim to the divine Augustus alone.

"I sing of arms and a man . . . ," he begins. Suddenly a hush falls over the vast room. The poet's deep, sonorous voice rings out. He launches into the thrilling tale of Aeneas, hero of the Trojan War, mythical founder of Rome.

At last he reaches the section of the tale where Aeneas and his band arrive at Carthage and are entertained at a banquet given in their honor by the resplendent Queen Dido. Aeneas, at the Queen's insistence, recites the tale of his tragic journey from Troy to the shores of Africa. "Rapt, she listened," the poet proclaims, "and the longer she heard him speak, the deeper she fell in love with him."

At the end of the end of our journey, we display our treasures. And the first of these is the story of the journey itself.

Like Virgil, we share our tale with those who assemble—loved ones who bade farewell to us when we left home, who welcomed us when we returned and kept us in their hearts all the time we were away. And as we tell our story, one by one the riches we brought back from our wanderings pour out.

Showing our treasures plays the journey through again. As we do, we notice that certain phases of the excursion that we might have thought insignificant come to the fore; areas of our story that we once believed to be the most consequential fade into the background.

Displaying what we have brought back is our way of making the tale more complete.

Each memento is a witness of where we have been.

Each time we bring a memento forth, it tells a fuller story of the journey.

And what it says is, "I sing of the epic quest . . . of bravery in the face of danger . . . of perseverance and kindness . . . of the exhilaration of self-exploration and discovery."

🐚 Share the Experience 🐚

Holding a party to talk about your trip and show what you have brought back would seem to be the easiest activity in the world. And yet, it has a deep meaning for the conscious traveler.

To approach this show-and-tell exercise with awareness, you may want to follow some simple steps.

The first has to do with timing. It is best to wait a few days, a week, or more before "going public" with your trip. The time between your homecoming and your telling of the tale is precious. During that time you will be resting from your recent experiences. You will be digesting, assimilating, and attaching emotional and spiritual priorities to all the things that happened while you were away from home.

When you feel you are truly ready, invite people over. You may want to do this as one big party or as several small ones. Whatever you decide, remember that it is important for you to bring complete closure to your journey by telling the story of it to others. Displaying the treasures you brought back is part of your storytelling.

Another benefit of this activity: your friends and family members will ask you questions as you proceed through your narrative and reveal your mementos. The interest of loved ones, and their comments, will help you see what is important in the story of your trip from another's point of view.

Nothing seals a journey like telling others about it. And nothing will bring you more satisfaction than sharing your adventures with those you love.

My journey has opened me to the most spectacular vistas of the spirit. I offer myself, transformed, to those who stayed at home . . .
In telling the tale of my travels, I am made complete.

The art of learning fundamental common values
is perhaps the greatest gain of travel to those
who wish to live at ease among their fellows.

—Freya Stark, *Perseus in the Wind*

To Find What Is Important

The revelers all have gone.

Strong shafts of morning sunlight pierce the deserted banquet hall.

We walk among the tables and the couches remembering how our voices echoed in this place last night. Here is where we stood and mesmerized the imperial household with the epic tale of our wanderings.

Now we are alone.

The story of the journey plays in our mind. The reciting of it has created something new in us. In telling the tale, we have begun to see our many exploits at a distance. From time to time during our oration, we felt that all these adventures might have been happening to another person.

In truth, the journey did happen to someone else—the person we once were but are not any longer. We have transcended the details of our travels. They have served us well. But now we are seeing the larger picture.

Like the world's great symphonies, our journey has had a theme.

Telling the tale has been a way for us to locate and understand that theme.

Perseus announces to his mother, Dana, and her prospective husband, the noble Polydectes, that he will produce the perfect wedding present: the head of the hideous Gorgon, Medusa. This will be no easy task, for anyone who looks into the face of the serpent-haired Medusa turns instantly to stone. To slay Medusa will take cunning beyond mortal ability.

The hero goes off into the dark land to seek and slay the dreaded Gorgon—this is the archetype of going within to search out our greatest fear, to confront it, and to overcome it.

Hermes, messenger of the gods, gives Perseus a shield lined with a mirror. Now he will be able to decapitate the monster without staring it in the face, by using the mirror as his guide and protection.

Heaven always offers help to the hero. Once we have decided to undertake the responsibility of re-creating ourselves, the entire universe moves to support our efforts.

For Perseus, slaying the Medusa of his worst fear was the theme of his mission. He was successful and returned to tell the tale, holding aloft the lifeless head of his fear.

Hercules, hero of heroes, is given the gargantuan assignment to perform twelve superhuman tasks. Among them is the purging of the Augean stables in a single day. The stalls hold thousands of cattle, and have not been cleaned for years. To perform this labor, he has to divert two rivers into the stables.

Metaphorically, the hero is called upon to rid himself of negative emotions and attitudes—and to do it quickly. The task is daunting, but he is up to it because of his resoluteness and inner strength.

Each of us is the hero of our journey.

Now we assemble the chapters of our tale to find the theme. For there is a theme to our travels, as surely as there was one for Perseus and Hercules and all the other heroes. Perhaps it is not something as grand as theirs—facing and overcoming our worst fears or confronting all that we find negative within us and washing it away in a Herculean purge. Our theme may lie in a simpler register: forgiveness, closure, retribution, duty, reunion, discovery, benevolence, responsibility, connection.

We locate the theme for our journey.

This is why we left home, why we sallied forth—and why we returned.

❧ A Simple List ❧

A myriad of experiences, tangles of people, a legion of emotions—your trip and its aftermath have been full and exciting.

After the gatherings with family and friends, during which you told the story of the journey, you at last have the luxury of some quiet time. This is the perfect time to articulate in a word or two what the trip was all about. Coming up with a motif for your travels is an exercise in mindfulness that lifts your journey firmly onto the spiritual plane.

Try this. List the people you encountered on the trip, and next to their names, write in a word or two describing your encounter with them. Review the words you have written. Do you see a pattern, a recurring theme?

Recently a friend of mine arrived home from a trip to the town of her childhood, which she had avoided for many years because, as a child, she had not felt accepted there.

When she sat quietly and did this exercise, she found herself writing down the words "friendly" and "kind" next to people's names. The words appeared so often that she concluded—rightly—that she had made the journey in order to heal her relationship with her own childhood.

Her theme: "Acceptance."

 I am the hero of my wanderings.

I go out and come back for a reason—and that reason is the theme of my traveling. In the theme are locked the lessons for which my soul is yearning.

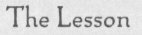

> *The real voyage of discovery lies not in discovering*
> *new lands but in seeing with new eyes.*
>
> —Marcel Proust

The Lesson

Now that we have discovered the overriding motif of our travels, we have the opportunity to learn the lesson that the journey offers us.

So, we ask, what is the lesson of this journey?

We ponder what the journey has taught us. On the wings of imagination, we fly back to the first suggestion of the journey in a dream. It was there that the seeds of change were planted.

Then the Voice said, "Go, the world awaits you. Go, and bring back what is missing in you. Go, and you will be transformed—healed, completed."

And now we see that the lesson of the journey was there at the beginning, in the gentle call to venture forth. But we needed to make the journey in order to own it.

Here, at the end of the end of all our wandering, is the lesson. We have returned, victorious, with this in hand.

The lesson is that spiritual quality which we did not have before the journey. It is the attribute of soul without which we faltered and floundered. In the absence of that spiritual gift, we were somehow incomplete. Now, through enormous effort, we possess it wholly, and we feel ourself coming into the fullness of our humanity.

Every traveler brings back a different lesson.

And every traveler brings back the same lesson, which is self-discovery.

❦ Let the Journey Be Your Teacher ❦

Once you locate the theme of your journey, it is not difficult to discover the lesson of the trip.

This exercise is an extension of the previous one. In that example, my friend was able to heal her relationship with her childhood—symbolized by the little town in which she grew up—by listing the people she had met on her trip. Next to each person's name (sometimes it was simply "the store clerk"), she wrote down one or two words to describe her encounter with them.

In her case, the overriding motif of the time she spent in her hometown was "Acceptance." That was her theme—a surprising and most pleasing one, particularly since she had expected just the opposite. The next step was to find the lesson of the trip. It would come naturally out of the theme.

After sitting with her list and mulling it over for some time, this is what she wrote at the bottom of the page: "I have learned from this trip to accept other people, to be open to their acceptance of me, and, most of all, to accept myself . . . just as I am."

For my friend, who had felt rejection from others early in her life and had internalized those feelings of rejection, learning this lesson represented an enormous emotional and spiritual breakthrough.

Your lessons from travel will be your own. They may not always be as profound as those of my friend, but they will present themselves, if you allow them. And when they emerge, they will comfort you and heal you.

The journey is your teacher—and you have been its willing student.

The lessons of this journey will stay with you forever.

 I weave out of the fabric of my wanderings a tapestry of teachings.

Everywhere I have gone, everything I have done, has been for this—the spiritual lesson that I now take within. Had I stayed at home when the journey called me, I would never have learned this lesson.

Gratitude fills my heart.

One could argue that a few individuals—sailors, fliers,
travelers, or mountaineers—while appearing needlessly
to expose themselves to danger and death may, in fact,
be unconsciously serving the interest of us all . . .

—Mary Russell, *The Blessings of a Good Thick Skirt*

The New Dream

The journey ends at the junction of another road.

And another journey begins.

Inner travel knows no dead ends, only new avenues opening onto fresh journeys.

We have told the epic tale of our mighty adventures. We have retired to this place alone and pondered the spiritual significance of our going out and coming in. The gods of travel have showered us with glorious insight, so that now we understand at last the reasons for our long sojourn in those far-off lands.

The journey has been our soul's teacher. It has taught us well; we have learned its lessons. And now we are home.

Inexorably, life proceeds. We absorbed all we have experienced, and we have been transformed by it.

The traveler who left home is not the same traveler who returned. We are different: we are new. And this newness is the higher throne from which we survey the enchanted countryside of our life.

Home.

For a moment, we believe that we will never leave here. For a moment, we imagine it would be madness to entertain abandoning the comforts of this blessed place.

We enter the garden as the sun is waning.

We sit in the shade and, after a time, we begin to drift into a blissful slumber.

The sky reddens around the furrows of the fleeing sun chariot. Still we sleep on, oblivious to the gentle lapping of the fountain, the sudden appearance of a cricket and a nightingale.

And now before us looms the angel of the journey, mute, its great wings barely moving in the evening breeze.

In the dream, we will greet this noble and powerful being. We have met before. Its quiet invitation to undertake a new journey will both excite us and inspire us.

We will be transfixed.

In the dazzling light from the angel's face, we will have forgotten the pleasant comforts of this kingdom—for we are beckoned on to new kingdoms, even finer and more radiant than this.

✿ Travel On ✿

You have completed your journey. Now you see that the arc comes full circle back to the beginning.

You have transformed yourself into a conscious traveler. By making your trip an archetypal journey, you have elevated it to a high spiritual plane.

The way of the conscious traveler is to see, hear, and feel every experience in the enchanted process of the journey.

You are the protagonist of your drama, the hero of your quest. You have been abroad on a mission, and it has been an expedition to reach the spiritual heart of yourself—there to be transformed.

Travel in the outer world is a metaphor for the journey inward. And the reward for this sacred sojourn is the spiritual gift of grace: the grace of peace, the grace of wisdom.

Now you are listening for the call of a new journey. When it comes, you will be ready.

You create a new travel shrine.

It is empty at the moment, awaiting the promise of a new journey.

The journey within has made me wiser and more powerful. Transformed, I wait in silence, in strength. Soon the gods of travel will call me forth again.

    And I will heed the call.

Recommended Reading

Throughout this book I have referred to classic works of travel literature by quoting passages from them. Here is a brief list of some of those books and a few others that I believe will support your interest in the spiritual aspects of travel.

Arabian Sands by Wilfred Thesiger, Viking Press, 1985. Sir Wilfred Thesiger's moving account of his journeys through the Arabian Peninsula.

Autobiography of a Yogi by Paramahansa Yogananda, Self Realization Fellowship, 1997. Originally published in 1946, this is one of the great classics of spiritual literature.

Bitter Lemons by Lawrence Durrell, Marlowe & Co., 1996. Although he is best known for *The Alexandria Quartet*, Durrell is an insightful writer on travel. *Bitter Lemons*, set in Cyprus, is one of his three island books, which also include *Prospero's Cell* (Corfu), and *Reflections on a Marine Venus* (Rhodes).

Brown Water Cafe by Bill Barrett, Owlseeall Publishing, 1998. A cross-country trip provides the setting for Barrett's reflections on our culture. This is a travel journal with a strong philosophical and spiritual thrust.

Greek Myths by Robert Graves, Penguin USA, 1993. A classic reference book on mythology for both the serious scholar and the casual inquirer.

Handbook for the Soul edited by Richard Carlson and Benjamin Shield; Little, Brown; 1995. Essays about how to nourish the soul by, among others, Lynn Andrews, Wayne Dyer, Robert Fulghum, Bernie Siegel, and Ram Dass.

Hard Travel to Sacred Places by Rudolph Wurlitzer, Shambhala Publications, 1994. A well-known novelist and screenwriter makes a life-changing journey through Cambodia, Thailand, and Burma.

The Hero with a Thousand Faces by Joseph Campbell, Princeton University Press, 1990. A classic, originally written by Campbell in the 1940s, about how myth inspires our lives.

India Seen Afar by Kathleen Raine, George Braziller, 1991. The third volume of Kathleen Raine's autobiography, in which she reflects on the "India of the Imagination—the term of every spiritual quest."

Mythology by Edith Hamilton, Signet Books, 1982. You might have encountered this book is grade school—and again in college. A world-renowned, popularly written compendium of myths.

Nothing to Declare by Mary Morris, St. Martin's Press, 1999. This 1988 travel memoir is filled with brilliant insights into both Latin America and travel in general.

A Path with Heart by Jack Kornfield, Bantam Doubleday Dell, 1993. Western Buddhist master Kornfield speaks about his personal, practical wisdom, based on twenty-five years of practicing and teaching the path of awakening.

A Return to Love by Marianne Williamson, HarperCollins, 1993. The internationally acclaimed author speaks on the rewards of bringing a spiritual dimension to our lives.

The Road Within: True Stories of Life on the Road edited by Sean O'Reilly, James O'Reilly, and Tim O'Reilly; Traveler's Tales, Inc.; 1997. Writers, among them Annie Dillard, Huston Smith, and Natalie Goldberg, speak of travel as an inner journey.

Sacred Journey by Eric Klein, Medicine Bear Publishers, 1998. Seeker Eric Klein writes about the nature of the spiritual path and about his spiritual unfoldment.

Sacred Journeys in a Modern World by Roger Housden, Simon & Schuster, 1998. A inspiring travelogue and spiritual journal.

Tacking the Serpent: Journeys to Four Continents by Janine Pommy Vega, City Lights Books, 1997. Poet Janine Pommy Vega searches for truth and self-realization in the far corners of the world.

D. H. Lawrence and Italy: Twilight in Italy, Sea and Sardinia, Etruscan Places by D. H. Lawrence, Penguin USA, 1997. For Lawrence, known mostly for his fiction, all travel tends to be inner travel.

What Really Matters by Tony Schwartz, Bantam, 1996. A journalist writes about his travels in search of learning what really matters in life.

Wind, Sand, and Stars by Antoine De Saint Exupéry, Harcourt Brace, 1967. For this master of lyrical writing, flight is a metaphor and a symbol of human aspiration.

Your Sacred Self by Wayne Dyer, Harper Paperback, 1996. These reflections on the spiritual core at the heart of human nature suggest that approaching life as a sacred event will enhance everything we do.

Acknowledgments

I would like to thank David Christian Hamblin for his contribution to the concept of this book, Tamar Stieber for suggesting the title, and Dianna Delling, my editor, for her considerable gift of clarity.

For their helpful advice and encouragement, I would also like to thank Snow Anderson, Hazel Archer, Chris Calloway, Cassandra Conyers, Colleen Craig, Diane DiRoberto, Monica Faulkner, Constance Higdon, Hal Isen, Pancho Kohner, Sabine Lucas, Dr. Margaret Olsen, Ron Savarese, Lupita Tovar, Renee Ziesing, and my literary representative, Barbara Neighbors Deal.

About the Author

Diane DiRoberto

JOSEPH DISPENZA has studied spirituality firsthand, living eight years as a monk—one of those years in total silence. He is the author of eleven other books and numerous articles on spirituality, and he is an accomplished public speaker on the subject.

For several years Joseph headed the education division of the American Film Institute and lectured in communication at American University in Washington, D.C. Later he established the successful Moving Image Arts program at the College of Santa Fe and taught courses in media ethics. He is the co-founder and director of the Parcells Center for Personal Transformation in Santa Fe, an institute that advances the philosophy of holistic healing.

Joseph welcomes correspondence from readers. You can reach him directly through the Parcells Center website: www.parcellscenter.com.